"Rejection so easily entangles us. It ___ ___ tional growth and trust in people, it t___ ___ and it becomes a mechanism of self-protection. This book offers wisdom in how to react to rejection and clearly shows how we can turn heartbreaking wounds into something purposeful and redemptive. Because rejection is inevitable, this book is a must-read!"

Lauren Scruggs, *New York Times* bestselling author,
wellness enthusiast, lifestyle blogger, and entrepreneur

"One thing is for certain: we need more voices like Kait's in the world, helping us navigate the hard-to-talk-about subjects like rejection, heartbreak, and insecurity. Unafraid to bring out the real talk (with a perfect amount of candor), Kait invites us into a bigger story of what life can look like when we stop avoiding the hard stuff and start fighting back. Don't be afraid to lean all the way into this book—you're in the best hands!"

Hannah Brencher, TED speaker
and author of *Fighting Forward*

"Kait's honesty and vulnerability will keep you nodding your head and turning the page. So many relationship books are written by married people who don't understand today's unique challenges. So many of them focus on just helping you find love. Kait has written a book that helps you look inward, deal with shame, and move forward with hope. If you've ever felt pain from love, Kait's story will help you find healing."

Jonathan Pokluda, host of the *Becoming Something* podcast
and bestselling author of *Welcome to Adulting* and *Outdated*

"Kait has written a phenomenal guide for taking radical ownership of our stories by showing us how to maximize the power that resides within our pain. Through no-holds-barred vulnerability and the willingness to tell the unfiltered truth about life's messiness, *Thank You for Rejecting Me* will show you how to live your boldest, bravest, and strongest life possible. My friends, this is a must-read!"

Mike Foster, author, counselor, and host
of the *Fun Therapy* podcast

"Kait flips the all-too-familiar relationship so many of us have with rejection. Instead of hating it, she teaches us, through her own story, that the rejection we (meaning every human being on the planet) experience on macro and micro levels every single day can be an access point to untapped growth, freedom, and God's presence. Thank you, Kait, for teaching us with grace and nuance that if we have the courage to press in, rejection can actually be one of our greatest allies."

Kat Harris, author of *Sexless in the City* and host
of *The Refined Collective* podcast

"*Thank You for Rejecting Me* smashes fear in the face with a fierce uppercut and will help you refocus on your promising future with God. You'll crack up at Kait's playful humor, but you'll also weep through some of her challenging stories and walk away thinking differently about your painful past. Grab this book!"

Rashawn Copeland, founder of I'm So Blessed Daily
and author of *Start Where You Are*

"Nothing holds us back like rejection. The memory of past rejection and the fear of future rejection cause us to live small and afraid—showing up as only a sliver of our full selves, revealing only a curated shell of who we really are. And in the process, we miss out on so much. We miss out on the beauty of being truly seen, known, and loved. We miss out on finding out who God created us to be. But in *Thank You for Rejecting Me*, Kait shows us how to break free from that crippling fear and step into true freedom. This book will change your life. I'm buying copies for every woman I know."

Stephanie May Wilson, author, podcaster, and speaker

"Rejection can either break you or remake you. Kait's story is a vulnerable, beautiful, humorous look into how heartbreak can be turned to hope. You'll laugh, you'll cry, and then you'll be challenged to see yourself as the woman God made you to be: beautiful, loved, and accepted just as you are."

Debra Fileta, professional counselor, creator
of TrueLoveDates.com, and host
of the *Love + Relationships* podcast

Thank You
for
Rejecting Me

Thank You for Rejecting Me

Transform Pain into Purpose and Learn to Fight for Yourself

Kait Warman

BakerBooks

a division of Baker Publishing Group
Grand Rapids, Michigan

Published by Baker Books
a division of Baker Publishing Group
PO Box 6287, Grand Rapids, MI 49516-6287
www.bakerbooks.com

Printed in the United States of America

Library of Congress Cataloging-in-Publication Data
Names: Warman, Kait, 1989– author.
Title: Thank you for rejecting me : transform pain into purpose and learn to
    fight for yourself / Kait Warman.
Description: Grand Rapids, Michigan : Baker Books, a division of Baker
    Publishing Group, [2021]
Identifiers: LCCN 2020035477 | ISBN 9781540900784 (paperback) | ISBN
    9781540901545 (casebound)
Subjects: LCSH: Rejection (Psychology)—Religious aspects—Christianity. | Self-
    acceptance—Religious aspects—Christianity.
Classification: LCC BV4905.3 .W37 2021 | DDC 248.8/6—dc23
LC record available at https://lccn.loc.gov/2020035477

This publication is intended to provide helpful and informative material on the subjects addressed. Readers should consult their personal health professionals before adopting any of the suggestions in this book or drawing inferences from it. The author and publisher expressly disclaim responsibility for any adverse effects arising from the use or application of the information contained in this book.

Some names and details have been changed to protect the privacy of the individuals involved.

Published in association with The Bindery Agency, www.The BinderyAgency.com.

In keeping with biblical principles of creation stewardship, Baker Publishing Group advocates the responsible use of our natural resources. As a member of the Green Press Initiative, our company uses recycled paper when possible. The text paper of this book is composed in part of post-consumer waste.

21 22 23 24 25 26 27   7 6 5 4 3 2 1

For my amazing *Heart of Dating* community.
I *never* would have had the courage to speak publicly
on these pages without you guys rallying behind me.
Thank you for listening, contributing,
sharing your own stories, and believing in me.
I truly consider you family.
We are in this boat together.

Contents

Foreword   11

Introduction   13
Not Today, Rejection

1. Neon Bikinis and Cellulite   21
Fighting Insecurity

2. Here I Am   41
Fighting Self-Hatred

3. Never Have I Ever   59
Fighting Sexual Shame

4. Sorry, Not Sorry   81
Fighting Not Fitting In

5. The Ugly Cry   99
Fighting Heartbreak

6. Now You See Me, Now You Don't   119
Fighting Abandonment

7. The Dreaded F-Word   137
   Fighting Failure

8. I'm Not Crazy   155
   Fighting Abuse

9. Big Little Lies   175
   Fighting Betrayal

10. All by Myself   193
    Fighting FOMO

11. Is This Thing On?   209
    Fighting the Silence of God

    Conclusion   229
    This Is Me

    Acknowledgments   239

    Notes   243

    About the Author   247

Foreword

We all have felt the sting and pain of rejection. Whether or not we want to admit it, we stuff emotions down and hide from the reality of what rejection sears into our psyche. Who wants to walk around with the label *REJECTED* written on their chest?

As a writer, teacher, and church leader, I have spoken to countless women in my years of ministry. I've listened to their stories and sat with them in their tears of grief, shame, and hurt, and I've found that the pain in these women's lives often started from a similar root: rejection.

When rejection happens, the last thing we need is a "Sweetheart, you'll be just fine" or *#blessyourheart*. We need true empathy. We need to feel seen, like someone else actually *gets* what it's like to go through the trenches. We need someone who is willing to walk alongside us.

Nothing is worse than revealing the depths of our pain only to have someone minimalize, trivialize, or offer a "simple" 107-step plan to perfect healing.

So where is the hope when it comes to facing this daunting thing called rejection? And who in the world is up for the task of helping us find it?

My girl Kait!

Over the years, I've had the honor of getting to know Kait personally, and I've witnessed how she walks through life as a single woman amid a myriad of heartbreaks and rejections.

Let me tell you, Kait isn't one of those women who runs away from the hard stuff. She also doesn't talk about things she has no idea about (like the well-intentioned pastor who tries to give dating advice even though they haven't dated in thirty years).

No, Kait is able to speak so passionately, so vulnerably, and so honestly about the painful topic of rejection because it's not lost on her. She's lived through rejection in some deeply painful ways. She's willing to go there. She guides you bravely and tenderly through her own story, allowing you to unlock your own pain to find healing and restoration.

Before this book, I didn't even think through all the ways rejection can come our way. We focus so much on external rejections, but have you ever thought about the ways we reject ourselves? Like how we disqualify ourselves before we even step into the ring? Or how we tell ourselves lies of insufficiency or let our insecurities eat away at us, affecting how we show up?

Kait reveals that even our most painful rejections are not wasted. But not only that, she displays how we can be free from their grip because of the powerful, healing love of God as he empowers us to find wholeness and restoration.

I believe we all long to be free. I believe even though rejection may continue to happen in some form, we all are desperate to find a place where we aren't crippled in the fear and anxiety of what might come next.

I'm so proud Kait is bravely leading this much-needed conversation, and I can't wait to see how her words change your life.

Bianca Juarez Olthoff, teacher, speaker,
and bestselling author

Introduction

Not Today, Rejection

I have a confession: for most of my life, I've been in a complicated relationship. Lord knows it hasn't been a fairy tale. *#thestruggleisreal.* Did the relationship make me feel good about myself? No, not really.

Actually, for most of my life I've wanted to walk away entirely. I wouldn't have called it love; it was probably closer to tolerance. I would've said, "Thank you, next" (Ariana Grande style) in a heartbeat if I'd had a choice.[1] But it's not quite that simple.

This whole relationship thing? Yeah, well, I guess it's less of a mutual relationship and more of an it-appears-always-uninvited-whenever-it-wants kind of thing, and I just couldn't seem to break free.

Maybe you can relate. I'd go so far as to say that you're in a similar relationship. The culprit?

Rejection.

I would bet everything I owned that if you're a woman reading this, you've had a complicated relationship with rejection too (and if you're a dude reading this, you're also welcome at this table, my friend). It can feel like a crippling sting trying to poison your life. Likely because of rejection, you've questioned some things about yourself.

My relationship with rejection has certainly led me down a path of uncertainty. I wondered, *Is anywhere or anyone safe? Will I ever be accepted just as I am? How will I survive if any of this happens again?*

Here's the hard news about rejection: we experience it almost every day—catastrophic bombs or minor pricks. Whether we like it or not, our stories are riddled with the sting of rejection.

We can be *so* confident until the rug gets ripped out from under us. We can show up brave and accepted, only to leave feeling unwanted and left out. We can do all the right things, open our hearts, and try our absolute best, only to end up completely heartbroken flat on our face. Whether it's within our families, our friendships, our dating relationships, our marriages, our bodies, our places of work or school, or even in the church itself—rejection seems to be waiting around every corner.

Ugh, there it is again.

As much as I wish I could take it all away, it's time to rip off the Band-Aid. You ready?

There's no magic trick to make rejection disappear forever. Life just doesn't work that way. Rejection will inevitably continue to happen to us; it is part of being human.

I know what you're thinking, This absolutely sucks.

I know we just met, but is it okay to talk to you as if we were already true eating-pizza-out-of-the-box-and-drinking-wine-in-our-sweatpants girlfriends? Because honestly, the conversations we are about to have in the pages of this book are anything but light and fluffy. The vulnerability I'm about to unpack would normally take me loads of time to share with a trusted friend. And while that partly terrifies me because many of these stories have never been told before, I also can't bear to think about you feeling the extreme weight of life's biggest rejections without experiencing a sense of hope for how you can grow through rejection. I can't bear that thought because, for me, so much of the pain in my life has come from rejection followed by seasons of stark hopelessness.

Just about every time I thought I belonged or believed I was chosen or felt certain I could do something or was convinced I had found "*my person*" or came to embrace the stretch marks and cellulite on my body, rejection came like a toxic ex-boyfriend with a mission to reinforce every terrible and crippling thought I've ever had.

I clearly don't belong here, or maybe anywhere.

I wasn't invited; they must not like me.

He suddenly broke up with me because I'm not enough (will I ever be?).

They turned me down, so clearly I'm a failure.

Maybe I deserve this treatment.

I'm flat-out ugly.

I can't trust myself, let alone anyone else.

Stable and secure love won't happen for me.

I should be ashamed of my sexual desire.

I've gained weight and am not desirable.

Honestly, I think I might hate myself.

God doesn't really care about me.

These thoughts didn't just sprout up out of nowhere. They reflect moments in time that haunt me. Chilling, unforgettable memories that have made a comfortable home in the crevasses of my mind, eager to pounce at any moment with their crippling negativity and doubt.

I know I'm not the only one.

Maybe you've doubted your self-worth and whether you're wanted or even likable. Or you've felt lost about where your future is headed. Or you've questioned your capacity to find people who really accept you. Or you've worked so hard to achieve something, only to fail. Or you've questioned your desirability, wondering if a man will ever choose you. Or you've been caught up in a web of deprecating thoughts about your attractiveness, and you constantly compare yourself to others. Or you've feared never finding secure and consistent love. Or you've wondered if you even like yourself. Maybe you've even found yourself questioning God, asking where he is in the midst of all this unthinkable pain.

And if you tell me you haven't felt even a sliver of any of the above, then please do me a favor and message me immediately with your incredible secret. You are, without a doubt, an anomaly. Bravo, darling. I encourage you to bottle that magic and sell it. Just make sure to call me when you do so I can invest in it (just kidding . . . kind of).

But if you're part of the 99.999 percent who have felt defined by your rejections, girl, am I ever with you.

Honestly? I'm fed up with being taken down, questioning everything about myself and my life all because of something I often cannot control: rejection. I am d-o-n-e, done.

I've had enough of the destructive aftermath that often follows rejection—the doubting, self-loathing, fear, shame, overwhelming pain and insecurity, and entire web of lies that roots itself in my mind like a bad weed. Those have got to go like the myriad of terrible exes I've said goodbye to. *Boy, bye.*

Are you with me?

Now, if we can come to accept that we aren't immune to rejection, and if we don't have control over anything but ourselves, then the big question is this: How can we get to the point where rejection may prick us, but it doesn't take us down entirely?

Well that, my dear, is exactly why I am writing this book.
Through these pages, let's together put a stake in the ground
and proclaim that while some form of rejection might continue to show up unexpectedly, we no longer have to be destroyed by it.

Rejection can try to have its way
with us, but that doesn't mean we
can't have our way with rejection.

> Rejection can try
> to have its way
> with us, but that
> doesn't mean we
> can't have our
> way with rejection.

Rejection shouldn't take us
down entirely.

Rejection shouldn't imply a lack
of success.

Rejection shouldn't determine our value.

Rejection shouldn't be a reason to quit.

Rejection shouldn't have the power to destroy our lives.

Rejection shouldn't be about *us.*

Instead, here's what I think rejection can be:

Rejection can build our strength and perseverance.

Rejection can be a stepping-stone to a new opportunity.

Rejection can clarify our purpose and calling.

Rejection can help us dive into wells of empathy and
compassion for those who are hurting.

Rejection can help us find a deeper, more secure love for
ourselves.

Rejection is a chance to turn to our most loving *God.*

Girl, it's time to reckon with your biggest life rejections. It's
time to bring them out of hiding and into the light. If we want
to live freely and wholly and wonderfully and purposefully, we

have to put on our big-girl panties and face one of the darkest forces in our lives. (Trust me, I know what it feels like to not want to move, but I know you can.)

Now, let me clarify one thing before we begin, okay? This is really important, and I want to make sure you don't miss it. This isn't a book solely filled with epic pump-you-up messages to make you feel less alone. While I do hope it makes you feel that way, I don't just want to cheerlead you and I don't just want you to walk away feeling encouraged and empowered. I want you to be equipped to move forward with freedom, fierceness, and tender, strong love.

You may have picked up this book with a toolbox that is a bit rusty at the moment, and that's okay. We might have to replace some of the tools, others we may have to dust off, and even others we will need to sharpen and make new again. But all I know is that we can't go into this battle against rejection without the best possible tools.

Think about it. Who wants to walk around saying, "This is the rusty toolbox I've been given, so I guess I just have to make do"? That is bonkers. You can do better than that.

I know you can!

You can do it. You can tap into deeper buckets of loving yourself. You can find strength to wholly heal from your darkest wounds. You can process your way through the ruins and step into the beautiful purpose God has waiting for you. And finally, you can access the resilience to face future rejections and not let them tear you down.

My biggest life rejections have made me into the woman I am today. They've led me to discover deeper parts of my soul, given me great endurance and profound strength, and helped me come face-to-face with hidden wounds and grimy shame to experience the tenderest, sweetest healing and love. They've also taught me how to stand strong in my identity as I've made peace with some, conquered and squashed others, and learned to settle the lingering fears about the rejections I might have to face in the future.

Body insecurity, self-hatred, loneliness, bullying, fitting in, abuse, sexual shame, betrayal, feeling like a failure, abandonment, heartbreak not knowing where God is in it all—we will talk about everything in this book, but with a determination that says, "Thank you for rejecting me; it's made me who I am today."

So, bust out a pen, a journal, your beverage of choice, and some tissues (just in case), and get comfy. It's time to love yourself just as you are, turn your hurt into hope, transform your pain into purpose, renew your tools, and fight for yourself like never before.

CHAPTER 1

Neon Bikinis and Cellulite

Fighting Insecurity

> One day I decided that I was beautiful, and so I carried
> out my life as if I was a beautiful girl. . . . It doesn't have
> anything to do with how the world perceives you. What
> matters is what you see.
>
> Gabourey Sidibe

Last year I went to the beach with my roommate, Kathleen.
I had asked her to be my ad hoc photographer for the day
because I had to take a few photos for a brand that sent me
an amazing box of products. Let me be clear: this was *not* a
swimsuit photo shoot. Not that there's anything wrong with
taking photos in a swimsuit, but this was just, er, not supposed
to be *that*.

The day of the shoot, I put on a swimsuit underneath my
beach outfit to make it seem less staged and more of a realistic

girl's day at the beach. I was feeling bold and opted for a neon-pink bikini that had been collecting dust in the back of my drawer.

What the heck, I thought. *No one's going to see me in this anyway.*

I had spent four beautifully hot, perfect, beach-weather summers living in LA and still hadn't had the courage to step out in a bikini.

After spending an hour carefully curating my "effortless," I-always-look-this-good-on-the-beach poses (never mind the ninety-five outtakes), we finally got the perfect shot. As we were packing our things away, preparing to leave, Kathleen stopped me.

"Kait, wait a second," she said. "Take off your shirt."

I didn't know whether to be horrified or to laugh hysterically. Take off my shirt for everyone to see me in my neon bikini top? I mean, I hadn't exactly chosen a subtle suit—this one was the color of highlighter pink and could be seen half a mile down the beach, not far from where an attractive man and his six-pack abs were reclining on a beach towel . . . yeah, I think not.

I quickly shot back at her, "Girl, absolutely not. Why in the world would I do that?"

I was inwardly pleading that she wouldn't bring up our recent conversation. You see, just one week prior, over late-night pizza and wine, I had shared about my desire to strip down the layers holding me back from seeing my body as truly beautiful. I wanted to wear less makeup, stop obsessively getting on the scale, and start owning the parts of my body that I had rejected. One of the things I specifically mentioned was—you guessed it—go to the beach and embrace my body in a bikini.

Then she said it. "Kait. We are not leaving here until you take off your clothes."

I laughed and sighed, incredibly reluctant to follow through.

Kathleen noticed my hesitation and insisted. "Kait, come on. Do it, girl! You know you want to. You've got this."

That was it, and I knew I had to go for it. "Okay," I said. "Let's do this."

And just like that, I slid off my lightweight oatmeal-cream sweater, revealing my not-so-toned, ate-fries-last-night-for-dinner stomach that hadn't seen the light of day in at least four summers. Just as I was about to unbutton my shorts, I stopped, drowning in the fears of being more exposed.

"Kaiiiiit. The shorts too. You can do this. Prove it to yourself. You are confident."

Was I, though?

I paused for a moment, closing my eyes and envisioning the woman I wanted to be: someone completely unashamed, comfortable in her skin, embracing her own definition of beauty. A flash of the amazingly confident and beautiful Alicia Keys without makeup at the 2019 Grammys crossed my mind.

That was it—the final bit of inspiration I needed. I knew what I had to do.

I unzipped my oversized denim shorts and threw them to the side like I was a famous singer changing backstage between acts.

There I stood—hot-pink bikini, untoned stomach, and thigh flab fully exposed for the lot of Los Angeles right there on Santa Monica Beach. I wanted to be able to smile and laugh as the camera clicked, feeling alive and free like those confident women in the ads. Everything was aligned, the ocean breeze tossed my hair ever so slightly, and one would think this was the perfect chance to strike a pose, smize (as Tyra Banks says), and be one with the camera—but I wasn't feeling the confidence coursing through my body . . . *yet.*

Plagued by Insecurity

Insecurity has played a bigger role in my life than I'd like to admit, and the roots run deep. I was the queen of brushing off insecurities, pretending they didn't exist, all while my sense of self and confidence continued to drown. It wasn't until I was instructed to draw out six of my most painful memories at Onsite, a therapy center outside of Nashville, that I was brought back to the memory of Christmas 2000.

I was eleven years old at the time. I had been gifted with the arrival of Aunt Flo a year earlier, and at the ripe young age of ten, I grew five inches and developed dark hair on my legs and my face erupted into inflamed, painful acne. I felt like a lone, gangly giraffe walking around my fifth-grade class. The cherry on top of this insecurity sundae? Braces.

That Christmas my family was gathering for a portrait and my Aunt Deb had set up our automatic Canon camera on a tripod. We posed, the camera clicked, and Aunt Deb stepped away from the group to review the snapshots. As she looked through the images, she made a comment I will never forget.

"Kaitlyn, why is it that when you smile, it always looks so fake? Can't you just smile normal?"

Her words made me feel like I was an ant crawling on the ground—small, embarrassed, and wanting nothing more than to disappear into any crack I could find on the ground. I wasn't trying to smile fake; I was just smiling as best as I could with my neon-banded braces. But something about the way I looked didn't sit well with her, and for whatever reason, she had to let me know.

Insecurity washed over me like a toxic flood. In that moment (and many more in the future), I became closely acquainted with something that would be a constant and unwelcome companion for years to come: body shame.

The fact that I didn't look like my idol Britney Spears didn't help either. How does one get such thin legs, perfectly toned abs, and shiny hair, anyway? My preteen self was confounded, and as I became more aware of the parts of myself that didn't match up, the shame and self-consciousness began to build.

Somewhere in those hormonally charged years that became chock-full of insecurity, I discovered the so-called gift of makeup. For me, makeup became the holy grail in trying to attain some seemingly perfect standard of beauty. Eventually, I couldn't go out without it. I created an elaborate routine to mask my insecurities, fearful of my bare face ever being seen. As a young teen at sleepovers, I would set an alarm and sneak to the bathroom before everyone was awake so I could carefully layer on makeup before slipping back into my sleeping bag, closing my eyes, and pretending to sleep until I awoke alongside the other girls, "face ready." I was doing everything to belong, feel pretty, and avoid the sting of rejection I had felt when Aunt Deb criticized my smile during that infamous family portrait. If how I looked wasn't okay, you better believe I was up for the challenge of curating the girl others seemed to want to see.

Into adulthood, the masking continued. I let shame dictate how I dressed so as to appeal to men. I carefully curled my hair in an attempt to stand out from the other gals. I continued to cake on makeup to hide my acne-scarred skin. I became cripplingly fearful of others noticing if I had gained any weight. God forbid if I had to go swimsuit shopping unless it was followed by a glass of wine (or three) to recover from the ensuing tailspin of feeling undesirable and unworthy.

My peers, my family, men, the media, words spoken over me, and the way I saw myself all influenced what I thought my body should look like and what I perceived true beauty to be.

In that transition from the girl we are to the woman we're becoming, our sense of self dramatically shifts. We become more aware of our appearance in relation to other women. We are influenced by female icons, what we see in the media, or even what the "popular" crowd around us looks like. Our differences feel exposing, like a liability we carry around. We're told what clothing will make us desirable and what we should or should not wear. We start caring about finding the perfect-size jeans that will hug and flatter our figure in all the "right" places. We become hyper aware of our curves, our best angles in photos, and how our hair, no matter what we do, just won't flatten, curl, or volumize like the hair of that one pretty girl we know.

Though I once ran free as an innocent little girl, growing into womanhood was fraught with confusion, comparison, self-loathing, insecurity, and body shame. My body that was wonderfully formed in my mother's womb had become something I hid more and more as I increasingly compared myself to others and clung to lifeless, untruthful words previously spoken over me.

Maybe something like this happened to you too. Maybe the narrative was a bit different, but the end result was the same.

Maybe you developed later in life and compared yourself to everyone else with curves and boobs, never feeling "womanly" enough. One of my best friends shared with me that at sixteen she was reading a magazine article about matching your style to your body type. She began to read off the types listed: pear-shaped, hourglass, apple, and then finally . . . boyish. Because she didn't have the same types of curves as other women, she felt as though she was assigned a cultural label telling her she had a body like a boy.

Maybe you feel ashamed of your curves and always jump on the train of the next diet—keto, anyone? Maybe you've been made to feel guys don't like women with a flat chest, so you wear the best padded bra you can find. Maybe you hate the uneven texture of your skin or the shape of your face and slather on tons of makeup to feel transformed into someone who feels "presentable." Maybe you feel like you have to have curves to the nth degree to be desirable, like the infamous Kardashians. Maybe you've struggled so desperately with your appearance and the insecurity has lodged so deeply that you've justified limiting or purging your food to the point of an eating disorder.

I've experienced more than one of these repercussions of letting insecurity define me. I bet you've experienced some too.

Insecurity, fear, and shame about myself, and specifically my appearance, began wreaking havoc on my life. I missed opportunities, I was riddled with anxiety, I self-sabotaged relationships with seemingly good men, and I acted out in jealousy toward other women. I rejected myself before anyone else even had the chance to reject me. And time and time again, I was left feeling empty, ashamed, and ugly.

> I rejected myself before anyone else even had the chance to reject me. And time and time again, I was left feeling empty, ashamed, and ugly.

Taking Back Our Power

My God-given identity that originally defined my body as beautiful, unique, and perfect just as it was had become a distant memory. Body shame had become so crippling in my life that I was forced to uncover where the self-rejection had originated and explore what it would look like to rediscover my inherent worth.

Here's the deal: in talking about our biggest rejections, we need to start by diving into the very thing that keeps us small and vulnerable. Insecurity (especially when it relates to our appearance) can not only lead us to reject ourselves but also leave us more susceptible to being fully knocked out when other life rejections come our way.

Girl, hear me out on this—our beings *and* our bodies are perfectly made by God. God shaped and formed them and said all of it was good (if you don't believe me, open up the Bible and read Genesis 1). But here's the thing: it's hard to move head knowledge (something we know to be true) into heart knowledge (something we practice in our lives). It's nearly impossible to find beauty and value in our bodies and our whole selves when we're constantly comparing and measuring them against culture's ever-changing standards.

The reality is, upwards of 90 percent of American women today are unsatisfied with their bodies, which is staggering and heartbreaking.[1] Whether we like it or not, our brains are constantly being hijacked by our culture's standards of beauty—which, by the way, have changed throughout time.

Our past and our personal stories create a deeply rooted narrative that influences how we feel about ourselves and our bodies. Pain and trauma, harsh words, the way approval has been extended to us or withdrawn from us—all that has created an incredibly convincing and toxic web of deeply ingrained beliefs about our bodies.

> It's nearly impossible to find beauty and value in our bodies and our whole selves when we're constantly comparing and measuring them against culture's ever-changing standards.

If you're fed up like I am with the superficiality and unreasonable standards forcing us into intense body shame, fear, and anxiety, I want to ask you this: What do you *want* to believe about beauty? How do you *want* to feel in your body?

Do you want your definition of beauty to be from the unrealistic or unattainable standards set by culture and media? Do you want your beauty ethic to be based on the ingrained internal messaging flashing in our brains from past hurts and traumas? Or do you want to redefine what beauty means to you and start putting boundaries in your life that reflect and honor this new ethic? Once you begin to deeply and fiercely fight to accept a new definition of beauty, you can then work to strip down the layers keeping you stuck in body rejection.

The ultimate question here is, Do you want to take back your power when it comes to the definition of beauty and how you see your body?

It's *your* choice.

Stripping Down the Layers

If you're anything like me, your internal dialogue might be swirling with thoughts that sound something like this: *I want to learn to love myself and my body for what it is. I really do, but for whatever reason, I just feel like I can't. How can I go about loving this vessel that I have learned to hate for so long?*

This is the crux of the matter. It's the ultimate question that's likely bubbling up in your soul right now. *How do I repair this relationship with my body?*

Mending our relationships with our bodies takes going through the piles of body shame and negative habits that have accumulated within us (often through a multitude of years and bad habits). Habits can be tough to break but not nearly as painful as continuing to live under the weight of body shame.

Years ago, I got into the habit of waking up every morning, lifting my shirt, analyzing myself from the front and then from the side, and immediately judging what I saw. Sometimes I didn't go out at night if I felt my body was too bloated. I didn't want to risk being seen, and I especially didn't want to take the chance of being in photos in which my face or body looked puffy and unmistakably rounder.

Eventually, this led me down an even more painful road of wanting to cover up my imperfections in a more extreme way: through the "art" of photoshopping.

Through an extensive Google session and a plethora of YouTube videos, I figured out a sneaky way to make simple edits to photographs that were barely noticeable—just enough to make sure my face and body shape looked slightly more toned and chiseled than they actually were. It didn't take long for me to become obsessed with making these changes before posting the picture on my blog or on Instagram. Much to my excitement, the app Facetune was soon released, making it even easier for me to pinch, tuck, and smooth just a few things on my face, legs, and arms. At the time, I justified the small tweaks. They were enough to ensure I felt more comfortable releasing images of myself into the world.

Why did I edit my photos? What was my true motivation? These are the questions I've been forced to face.

Can we be honest-to-goodness real about our intentions when it comes to how we act toward our bodies? What are we looking to get from or hide from others? We hold the remote to whatever narrative is playing in our minds—only we can know our true motivation.

I want you to be real about the tendencies and mindsets that fuel your insecurity. What are you doing to conceal, conform, or change your body? What negative thoughts do you believe about your body, or what lies have you heard that affect how you see yourself? What do you believe you'll gain if you "perfect" the appearance of your body according to society's standards?

As I mentioned before, here are some of the behaviors I noticed in myself:

- Covering my face with layers of makeup
- Never, ever wearing a bikini
- Editing my body to look flawless for social media
- Obsessively doing squats and lunges and extreme workouts
- Staying at home when I was bloated, and especially never being in pictures while out

Now, let's talk about the motivation behind my behaviors:

- Covering my face with layers of makeup *to display a flawless outward façade*
- Never, ever wearing a bikini *for fear of exposing all the areas I thought weren't perfectly toned*
- Editing my body for social media *so I could portray an idealized version of myself*
- Obsessively doing squats and lunges and extreme work-outs *to create the body I believed others wanted to see*
- Staying at home when I was bloated, and especially never being in pictures while out *to hide my puffy body*

And because we are already deep into this hole, let's also call out the fear driving these motivations:

- I am not pretty enough to be liked.
- I am not skinny enough to be desired.
- I am not accepted for who I really am.
- I am not fit enough to stand out and be considered.
- I am not perfect enough to be loved.

Well *that* was exposing but necessary. If we don't look at the patterns that have left us stuck under body shame, we won't be able to walk in our true beauty and live in the actual freedom of loving our bodies.

Our bodies are true miracles. They are marvelous wonders that allow us to gracefully and poetically

If we don't look at the patterns that have left us stuck under body shame, we won't be able to walk in our true beauty and live in the actual freedom of loving our bodies.

dance, have athletic stamina and strength, think deeply and invent life-changing ideas, and experience the flavor of life through our senses. What if we peered beyond the outer appearance we're trying to present to the world and saw that what we really want is to feel a sense of belonging, acceptance, love, and connection?

Can I tell you something? Perfecting, masking, excessive dieting, hiding, extreme editing—they will always show up empty-handed. They will never deliver on those things.

Confidence is healthy and true and good and something I deeply believe God wants us to have. Sure, he doesn't want us to walk with pride, thinking our bodies are better than everyone else's (that's comparison, part of what got us into this mess in the first place). Rather, he wants us to live with the pure confidence that we were inherently created as beautiful, that our bodies are magnificent, and—ultimately—that we are deserving of love and belonging.

Genesis 1:27 says that God created us in his image. As we were being formed in our mother's womb, each part of us was created uniquely, with meaningful, special flare.

Because of this, our confidence does not have to come through external validation. Rather, our confidence can come from the divine source of our creation.

Friend, your beauty is inherent. Your body is magnificent. Don't you want to believe that at your core as truth?

As we carve out a deep love for our bodies, stripping down the layers that caused us to embrace a false sense of worth, we can begin to walk in pure confidence without the need for outside people and influences to affirm our worth.

But don't be naive. Lies about our bodies will still seep into our minds. Influences about what is and is not beautiful will still do their best to persuade us. People might say mean things or cast judgment about our looks. And because of all this, you absolutely must come prepared in strength and truth to fight against any form of body shaming.

After stripping down the layers and stepping into true confidence, I realized I had to be extra careful to protect my new-found love for my body.

Here's what helped me:

1. *I became extra critical of the media I consumed.* When it came to social media, I had to be brutally honest about what was drawing me away from healthily loving myself and my body. This meant questioning who I was following and why I was following them. In the process, I ended up unfollowing a whole bunch of accounts that did not support my journey or that promoted any sort of "ideal" body image. Instead, I began following more life-giving, empowering, body-diverse accounts. I also started paying attention to the messaging I was receiving in all media I consumed as it related to weight, body, food, and beauty. Pay attention to what you are looking at, challenge what you see as harmful, and put protective boundaries in place to safeguard your mind.

2. *I started listening to the messages my body was giving me.* Oftentimes we treat our bodies like a thing and not a living being. We neglect to feed ourselves, we don't rest when we need it, and we don't pause to listen when we feel aches or pains or tensions. In the process of staying connected to my new definition of beauty, I started listening as I would to someone who was important to me. When my body was hungry, I ate. When it was tired, I rested. When it felt tension or anxiety, I pressed in, trying to pinpoint why, and did what I needed to do to take care of it. I'll be honest, this one was incredibly

hard being the workaholic that I am (more on that later), but staying the course has transformed my relationship with this beautiful vessel of mine. Treat your body with the respect it deserves and you'll begin to feel more connected, like you're in a mutually valuable relationship.

3. *I started doing things that connected me to my body.* I began dancing more (awkward dance moves and all). I started practicing breathwork. I began to box. I spent more time meditating. I took regular baths. I went on walks in the sunshine. I dove into the ocean. What makes your body feel happy and good? Do more of that.

4. *I began hanging around people who also love their bodies.* This one is really important. I think it's true that we often become who we spend time with. We are deeply influenced by what others say about us, but we are also influenced by what others say about themselves. Our brains can pick up on even subtle messaging, so we have to be aware. Do your friends encourage you to love your body? And do they also practice that themselves? Be around people who are on the journey with you and are committed just as much as you are to working through insecurity versus sitting in it.

The path to body acceptance and a truly filled, meaningful life is not earning our worth through our appearance. We can see ourselves as beautiful, *and* we don't have to let our external appearance dictate our full identity—it's part, but not all, of who we are.

From one struggling-to-love-her-body-exactly-as-it-is woman to another, I just want to say this: *you are enough.* Your appearance doesn't grant you access to true love and belonging. You are no less valuable, lovable, or gorgeous if you weigh more or if you weigh less. Your body is beautiful just because it is, because God made it that way. You are beautiful just because you are, because God made you that way.

Oh, and that day on the beach?

As I stood there at first, skin exposed to the world in my neon-pink bikini, I felt anything but free. Yes, I wanted to be someone who was completely unashamed, comfortable in her skin, and able to embrace her own definition of beauty, but at that moment tinges of insecurity were stunting me. But something started to shift as I felt the sun on my skin and the breeze lifting my hair. I took a deep breath and began thinking less about how I was viewed or evaluated by others on the beach or even by my roommate, Kathleen. The awkwardness still lingered, but I started moving my body and posing for the shots, laughing at the absurdity of it all. Some may say I did my best "fake it until you make it" bikini photo session, but what I was really doing was showing insecurity who's boss.

> Your body is beautiful just because it is, because God made it that way. You are beautiful just because you are, because God made you that way.

There it was. I finally felt free and good and connected to my body. I felt what it was like to move and think less about how I was potentially being viewed, and just *be*—something I hadn't experienced in a long time. Not since I was that carefree little girl who hadn't yet faced the hormones and the comments from people like Aunt Deb and the constant inundation of what a woman "should" look like. Not since I had decided to be the girl the rest of the world wanted.

Before we left the beach that day, Kathleen had one more request for me. She said, "Kait, now look at these photos and say three nice things about your body." I begrudgingly took the phone out of her hands. I found the courage to strip down the layers and freely pose for the camera, but did I have the strength to change what I actually thought about myself?

I looked at the photos, and it was as though something clicked inside me. The practice of freeing my body on that beach had given me permission to unlock a newfound acceptance for myself. I looked down at the photos and was able to see the fullness of myself—the pain I carried but also the joy I felt at choosing to let go of insecurities and body shame, choosing to love the person I am in the body God gave me. I saw myself as a whole person, not just how I measured up against some arbitrary ideal.

I'm still a work in process. Sometimes I still like to wear a lot of makeup, but more and more these days I find myself walking outside with an Alicia Keys–type confidence, embracing my own invisible cloak that says "My name is Kait. I am beautiful, and my body is enough—exactly as it is."

Dear Body,

Hello, lovely. I had to start off by saying you are lovely, because what I have come to realize is that you are truly lovelier than lovely.

But here's the deal. I know I haven't treated you like you are lovely.

In the past, I was the worst friend to you. If I were you, I would have given up on me a long time ago. But here you are, standing strong, loving me anyways, giving me a way to continue on living this gift of a life. When I really think about it, you have shown me what it looks like to never give up on someone despite their constant wrongdoings. You've taken the hits of rejection time after time. You've never abandoned me, and for that I am brought to tears.

It's long overdue, but I have to say it now: I am so very sorry. From the bottom of my heart. I am sorry for hating you. For hiding you. For speaking poorly about you to others. For resenting you. I am sorry for treating you like an enemy. For comparing you to others. For voicing every single flaw.

Today I want to thank you.

Thank you for my smile. Thank you for my love handles that make me feel feminine. Thank you for my stretch marks that show I've lived a lot of life. Thank you for my unique face shape. Thank you for my green eyes. Thank you that I became a woman exactly when I was supposed to. Thank you for my legs that have taken me places every day, even when I felt they were ugly.

The thing I can finally see is that you are beautiful just the way you are. Thank you for being you.

Yours Truly,
Kait

Remember These Things

> ⟫ Ninety percent of women today are unsatisfied with their bodies, which is staggering and heartbreaking. Your brain is constantly being hijacked by the culture's ever-changing standards of beauty.

➤ Your body is a marvelous wonder that allows you to gracefully and poetically dance, have athletic stamina and strength, think deeply, invent life-changing things, and experience the flavor of life through your senses.

➤ Your appearance doesn't grant you access to true love and belonging. You are no less valuable, lovable, or gorgeous if you weigh more or if you weigh less. Your body is beautiful just because it is, because God made it that way. You are beautiful just because you are, because God made you that way.

Ask These Things

➤ What do you currently believe about beauty? What elements (i.e., media, culture, things people have said, etc.) comprise your belief system?

➤ How do you currently see your body? What do you struggle with most, and what has most influenced this view of your body?

➤ What would it look like for you to define beauty not according to culture, media, your past, or even your peers but rather distinctly in keeping with God's definition of how he sees *your whole self*, including your body?

Do These Things

➤ Create a new statement of belief about your beauty and your body.

➤ Check your motivations by (1) writing down five things you are doing to conceal/change your body, (2) recording the motivations behind each one of these things, and (3) naming the fear associated with each of these actions.

➢ Start walking with Alicia Keys–type confidence by (1) being critical of the media you consume, (2) listening to the messages your body sends, (3) doing things that connect you to your body, (4) hanging around people who also love their bodies, and (5) writing a thank-you letter to your body.

CHAPTER 2

Here I Am

Fighting Self-Hatred

If you had a person in your life treating you the way you treat yourself, you would have gotten rid of them a long time ago.

Cheri Huber

"I hate that version of myself. I don't want to go back there. I'm a new person today."

These were the words I uttered to my therapist, Lynne, during the Healthy Love and Relationships Program at Onsite, the therapy center I mentioned earlier. We had just been asked to complete an exercise called "the window pain." Key word: *pain* . . . yikes. Doing anything with the word *pain* in it doesn't exactly make you jump for joy. I quickly realized that Onsite's approach to healing and growth (my reason for attending the weeklong retreat) was not for the faint of heart.

I was instructed to take a giant poster board, split it into six sections (like a window pane), and draw out the six most painful memories from my childhood. Lynne noticed the look of panic on my face and proceeded to dump markers onto the floor in front of me.

I desperately wanted to tell her I was incapable of doing anything of the sort because I was a terrible artist and couldn't draw worth poop. But alas, I knew no excuse would grant me a get-out-of-jail-free card in this situation. After all, no one signs up for a week of intensive therapy without knowing they're going to have to do some uncomfortable (and at times painful) digging. I couldn't cheat my way out of this. Diving into the depths of my pain was downright unavoidable.

I stared at the blank, white poster board in front of me. Revisiting hurt and trauma from over two decades ago wasn't an easy task, and though part of me would rather have given up chocolate for the rest of my life, I needed to take the first step and be brave.

Sigh. Okay then, *fine.*

As I picked up a purple marker, I heard my inner cheerleader chiming in with words from the vulnerability master herself, Brené Brown. *Kait, "authenticity is a collection of choices that we have to make every day. It's about the choice to show up and be real. The choice to be honest. The choice to let our true selves be seen."*[1]

Even though you're terrified, I added, consoling myself.

Who doesn't want their inner enthusiast to sound like Saint Brené, am I right?

Let me tell you what: it's never easy diving into something you've worked tirelessly to minimize, stuff down, and hide from.

As I pressed through the visceral pain in my gut and pressed the purple crayon to the paper, I watched as my tears splattered against the poster board. As I drew, the stream of tears continued, and I faced some of the most prominent memories that had covered up my childlike innocence and sent me into a broken identity of doubt, shame, and self-hate.

It can hurt like heck to dive into the depths of our past, face the reasons we've learned to hate ourselves, and find a way to heal, but it can also destroy us a whole lot more to hold on to our pain and never let go.

> It can hurt like heck to dive into the depths of our past, face the reasons we've learned to hate ourselves, and find a way to heal, but it can also destroy us a whole lot more to hold on to our pain and never let go.

I really wished they'd prepared me for emotionally painful *#adulting* arts and crafts projects in elementary school. I'll never think of a poster board the same way again.

The Window Pain

Picture yourself as a young, innocent girl standing in a beautiful white room. Maybe you're four, maybe you're seven—whatever age comes to your mind first, stick with it. As you envision yourself standing in this room, notice your countenance. Maybe you have a slight smile on your face. Maybe your eyes sparkle with playfulness and wonder for the world that awaits. Maybe you're radiating peace, love, and joy.

Can you envision it?

Now try to remember the first difficult memory you can recall. It doesn't have to be something catastrophic. Maybe it's a small, seemingly inconsequential moment that impacted you so much that you can still recount every detail. Maybe it was a word you were called when you were five. Maybe it was a time someone did something to you that made you feel ugly or unwanted or not enough.

Do you have the memory? Picture that moment and stick with me.

Now I want you to envision a sheer, pink scarf getting thrown over your sweet little-girl self. It may be slightly jarring but not all that terrible, because pink is a pretty color, after all. Plus, it's sheer, so you can still see the outline of yourself underneath.

Next, I want you to recall another difficult moment. Maybe it's a time you felt forgotten or unheard. This time I want you to envision a sheer yellow scarf being thrown over your younger self. You can still see her underneath, but the outline is becoming a bit fainter now.

Then recall another hard moment you experienced. Maybe it was a time when you did something wrong and got punished or felt ashamed. Yet another scarf is thrown on top of the first two, and this time it's gray. It's becoming a bit harder to see your child self now, but trust me, she's still there.

Maybe you remember spending a night questioning the validity of your own thoughts and feelings. Or maybe you felt left out or different from all your friends. That's it—now picture a sheer blue scarf getting thrown on top of the pile.

Now let's pause and think. What's really happening here? These thin, barely noticeable scarves are starting to pile up, hiding your true self. They are building up until you are so covered by painful situations and moments of doubt, loathing, and shame that your little-girl self is barely visible underneath all the layers.

Maybe your childhood was filled with trauma, causing a multitude of scarves to cover you, or maybe your childhood wasn't actually all that bad. Maybe your parents were amazing, but subtle, difficult messaging or your interpretation of events began to diminish your sense of self. Eventually the layers became so prominent that you reached a point where your true self was hidden. All the layers covered who you were made to be.

These light, seemingly harmless scarves are actually something much more serious: little bits of shame. They are *shame scarves.*

This is exactly what can happen in the building up of our own self-hatred.

Your inner child is the part of you standing in that white room covered in shame scarves. It's the part of you that was hurt, betrayed, or forgotten over time but that still resides in your subconscious. Some of us ignore our inner child, maybe because we were so used to being invalidated and ignored. A lot of us react with extreme emotion and are unaware that it's actually all coming from the place of our inner child. And many of us, including me, try to shame our inner child, claiming we walk as a "new person" today because "that version of me was so 1999."

Today I want to challenge you to be aware that, under all those shame scarves, your inner child is part of you. The part of you that was vulnerable to hurt and pain is still there, connected to the core of your being.

Underneath it all, there's innocence and wonderment and creativity and purity—a part of you that's wholly and perfectly lovely. But that part of you is waiting for you to see her and, most importantly, accept her.

Facing the Shame

After drawing out my painful memories from childhood, Lynne invited me to connect with my inner child. But when I pictured that part of me, a young girl covered by all the scarves, I saw a version of myself I didn't like. I saw someone who had frequent angry outbursts and who was controlling, mean to other girls, constantly throwing fits, selfish, and dramatic.

There I was in that plush, carpeted room at Onsite, resisting Lynne's prompt. *I hate that version of myself. I don't want to revisit her. I'm a new person today,* I thought.

I continued my case, insisting that I didn't feel it was necessary to talk about how I was as a child, because I was a "changed woman now." The pain of revisiting memories, feelings, and *myself* as a child felt unbearably difficult.

But deep down, I knew the truth. If I was going to heal from something as deep-rooted as self-hatred, I couldn't walk around it, over it, or away from it. I was going to have to face the painful parts of myself that I thought I had left way back in the past.

I tried my best to push past the awkwardness and apprehension. I took a deep breath and grabbed ahold of any sliver of courage I could find floating around in my mind.

Lynne encouraged me to give myself permission to go back to my memories and just feel the feels. She explained that it didn't necessarily matter how dramatic an event seemed on paper, it was about how much it stuck with me and how I felt within it. She encouraged me to recall a specific situation and ask myself these two questions:

How does your adult self feel about this situation now?

How did your inner child feel about this situation when it was happening?

Remember that white room we talked about? Try to imagine your little-girl self there, and work to identify the shame scarves that were thrown over you through the years.

Self-hatred doesn't always come in one fell swoop. It can accrue in increments over time. Seemingly inconsequential experiences that appear almost forgettable at first start to slowly and sneakily pile up, covering our childlike innocence.

There are big-T traumas and little-t traumas. Both can happen, and both can feel painful and confusing and wreak havoc on our identity and our ability to love ourselves.

Did a big-T trauma happen? Maybe it was a little-t trauma? Was it a mix of both?

Expose the painful moments. Stare them dead in the face. Then ask yourself the same questions Lynne asked me:

How does your adult self feel about this situation now?

How did your inner child feel about this situation when it was happening?

You might experience a bit of resistance. This is normal. It's what happened to me. Once I let myself look at who I was—that girl underneath the pain and sadness—and set aside the shame and embarrassment I carried about that part of me, I felt my heart tugging, wanting to reach out and hug her, wanting to show her hurting heart some semblance of love, wanting to rescue her from the weight that had been put on her, but the fear was still too overwhelming.

I felt myself pull back, slipping into this automatic response: *Honestly, I don't want to look at her. She represents all that I've worked so hard to change. I'm not that girl anymore.*

Lynne grabbed a sheer rainbow-colored scarf with sparkles, and in a symbolic gesture, she threw it onto the pile of scarves in front of us that represented the shame that covered my inner child.

"This scarf represents your perfection and performance, Kait. It's what you've used to cover and mask what you are really feeling underneath it all. How do you feel seeing this?"

I quickly replied, "Well, at least that scarf is pretty."

Immediately, I could hear my inner Brené Brown coach saying, *Stop avoiding, Kait. Choose courage over comfort.*

Ugh . . . *FINE, Brené, fine.* The ping-pong match happening in my brain was certainly giving me a run for my money. It was time to really courage up and be honest about what the deepest parts of my soul were actually telling me.

"You know, I don't really like knowing that she has to hide under all of that. It must feel really lonely. Maybe even a bit scary. I guess if I'm honest, I'm a bit sad for her," I said to Lynne.

The Search for Self-Compassion

I finally took the first step toward acknowledging my inner child and being honest about my underlying feelings, but I still needed to find a place of deep compassion for her. Compassion is a key ingredient for the remedy of self-hatred.

To do this, I actually had to picture what my inner child was feeling about how I, adult Kait, saw her, hid her, and acted toward her.

I imagined that I was my younger self, hearing the words I had spoken to Lynne: *"Honestly, I don't want to look at her. She represents all that I've worked so hard to change. I'm not that girl anymore."*

Thankfully, I've never taken a physical knife to the gut, but I imagine if I had, it would have felt piercing like that. I was painfully coming face-to-face with my own self-hatred (something I had worked hard to avoid). There I was, head-to-head with all the reasons I loathed myself. All the ways in which I was selfish, all the people I couldn't impress, all the times I yelled and screamed in fits of confounded fury, all the moments I tried to control and manipulate, all the times I pinched others to make them feel inferior, all the childhood girlfriends I was mean to, all the ways I felt unheard by my friends and family, all the instances when I thought my parents didn't care about me.

The knife dug deep—to every last painful thing I had been stuffing under layers of anger and mounds of shame and topping off with shiny layers of performance and perfection.

My heartbroken soul cried out with a hot flood of tears and loud sobs. This was the moment Lynne had been guiding me to. A moment to experience the real feelings that existed under all the layers of self-loathing: an understanding that the little girl inside of me was lonely and hurting. She felt forgotten, unheard, different, never enough. And because of that, she lashed out in anger and with attempts to control. She tried to make herself feel valuable to others through performing and perfecting, and when it didn't work, she got louder. That little girl acted out because she didn't feel seen, heard, or loved.

All she wanted was to know someone really cared for her, saw her, heard her, understood her. She just wanted someone—anyone—to embrace *all of her.*

And just like that, I received my first dose of what felt like the most magical, healing emotion: compassion.

With tears in my eyes and my heart gripping on to empathy, I envisioned the scarves covering up my inner child and screamed, "This isn't fair!" A wave of angst came over me as I yelled out, imagining myself removing the scarves from my symbolic inner child—removing what she was never designed to hide beneath.

And there she was staring back at me—the deepest part of my soul exposed. Sweet innocence, pure love, the girl God so perfectly and originally designed who had been suffocating under layers of self-rejection. She was finally . . . *free.*

I fell to the ground sobbing. I imagined putting my arms around her, softly whispering, "Oh, love, I am so sorry. None of that should have ever happened to you. None of it was fair."

It really wasn't . . . fair, that is. The things that happened to us in our childhood that stole away our innocence. The messages we received that destroyed our worth and value. The ways our rights were violated or our needs were not met that caused us to shrink down, compartmentalize, hide, or act out, leading us to feel even deeper shame.

None of it was fair. We were never built to carry a weighted blanket of self-hatred. But unless we courageously dig through the layers, and unless we can find a dose of self-compassion, our true identity will suffocate under the layers. And ultimately, we will show up already rejected by the world, claiming that painful experiences have given us a permanent, irreparable identity.

What will it take for you to connect with your inner child, the inner parts of your soul, and find a sense of compassion?

Part of this process means identifying your typical numbing mechanisms. You've come this far—so don't stop. It's time to be honest with yourself. Your numbing mechanisms are your vices. You know, the things that are fun or distracting but that take you away from facing the shame scarves from your past.

> We were never built to carry a weighted blanket of self-hatred. But unless we courageously dig through the layers, and unless we can find a dose of self-compassion, our true identity will suffocate under the layers.

Here's the deal with numbing: it can feel natural and nice in the moment, but it will only prevent you from confronting your shame and keep you further from your inherent, beautiful identity.

My number one numbing vice has been performing. You might describe it as working, shape-shifting, people-pleasing, and trying to be the best at everything I do.

Maybe your vice is performing too. Or maybe it's drinking or spending money or constantly staying busy or mindlessly scrolling social media or excessively dieting or working out or spontaneously adventuring or being in control or isolating or helping others or having sex.

What is keeping you from facing what you don't like about yourself? What are your own colorful scarves that mask what's really living in your soul? How are you avoiding the hard things in life? What do you turn to in a moment of hardship?

Only you can identify it.

But let me tell you what: I'm pretty positive that between you and your numbing vice, an innocent, deep part of your soul is aching for your attention, waiting for you to gently care for, love, and accept her.

Choosing Connection

Discovering a taste of self-compassion can feel like dipping your toes into a bath of perfectly heated water. It feels so comforting, soothing . . . just right. But the journey to immerse yourself completely in the waters of compassion takes a series of courageous decisions.

Listen, I'm a thirty-one-year-old grown woman, and I just realized that an inner child exists within me, that I typically perform to keep her small, and that it's possible to find compassion for her. But even still, it doesn't mean I'm perfectly connected to her every single day. Unexpected things happen, I get heartbroken, I react defensively in anger when something triggers me just right. I make decisions to fill voids in my heart that are based in fear and feeling unworthy.

My mind doesn't automatically go where it's never been before. But now that my feet have finally discovered the path to the waters of self-compassion, it's easier to find my way back there. Now that I've tasted freedom and practiced showing up for my inner child, I'm more capable of walking down that road again the next time a shame scarf tries to keep me small and hidden.

This process isn't linear for me, and it won't be for you either. There are going to be days when you slip back into self-loathing. There are going to be times when you get triggered and react from the brokenness of your hurting, inner child. It's not *if* it happens, but *when* it happens. And when it does, you have to pull your best Muhammad Ali move and block the shame scarves being thrown in your direction.

After I finally found compassion for my inner child, I knew I had to break in this new path and make it playful. So I began to consistently connect with and love on that inner child I had identified at Onsite. As Christopher K. Germer says, "A moment of self-compassion can change your entire day. A string of such moments can change the course of your life."[2]

Here are a few things that worked for me:

- I started more regularly planning activities that allowed me to freely be as childlike and joyful as my heart desired. Since I'm in SoCal, I made a few trips to Disneyland. I also did other activities I loved as a child, like crafting.

- I took up coloring, immersing myself in creativity as I scribbled colors between the lines.

- I began reading novels—because my brain desperately needed a break from self-help—and got lost in all the fun stories and imagery.

- I started practicing guided meditation to instill a habit of quieting my mind. Meditation helps us better connect to the inner workings of our complex and beautiful souls. (For anyone who feels skeptical, meditation is not just for yogis and New-Age spiritual folk who wear boho clothes and have dreamcatchers around their house . . . those are unhealthy stereotypes. Meditation is a process of focusing our minds intently on something calm, positive, and good. Think of it as practicing Philippians 4:8, leaning in to whatever is true, noble, right, pure, lovely, admirable, excellent, or praiseworthy. Meditation is intentionally focusing on the good while calming our swirling thoughts, and it is something we can and should practice, following the way of Jesus.)

What childlike things can you do to connect with your inner child? What can you do to practice paying attention to the vulnerable parts of yourself? How can you start speaking to her (and in essence to yourself) with more love and compassion?

You have more control over your daily practice of self-love than you think. Fighting self-hatred and finding self-love are anything but linear. We never "arrive" at some perfect, ever-sustaining level of self-love. It's not a destination; it's a journey. And not only that, but this process looks different for every person.

It's not "Do this every day and you will experience eternal happiness" or "Make these moves and live the good life forevermore."

I don't pretend to know what unique things happened to you or offer a one-size-fits-all plan to discover self-love at the cost of self-hatred. Addressing the topic of self-hatred and the journey to reverse all the things that got you there could be an entire book all on its own. But we also can't truly talk about rejection without facing the biggest way we self-reject: through our own self-hate.

It takes time to sort through the reasons we hate ourselves so that we can more fully experience God's glorious love. It's a continual process, but it's also essential for our flourishing. If we don't fight for healing and fight to love the totality of ourselves, we'll never be able to identify, break down, and grow through rejection. And what a tragedy that would be, because on the other side of self-hatred is an exquisite beauty that comes from living in the fullness of our identity. It's merely waiting to be uncovered by you.

> On the other side of self-hatred is an exquisite beauty that comes from living in the fullness of our identity.

My experience at Onsite changed my life. But it doesn't have to take a fancy therapy retreat to face the shame and self-hatred you've been carrying. You can start taking the first step to self-love by becoming aware of your inner child right this very moment. Seriously, like right now. No more excuses. Are you ready to step away from the consuming waters of self-hate?

What is it going to take for you to admit that the disparaging ways you see yourself are poisonous and infect all sorts of areas of your life?

What is it going to take for you to reach a breaking point, recognizing that you're ready to live with newfound freedom and joy?

What is it going to take for you to live into the fullness of who you were created to be?

What is it going to take for you to gain the courage to connect to your inner child and start sorting through the things you don't like about yourself?

And as you mentally start digging to connect with the emotions of your soul, don't forget to put on your cape of courage. Picture me saying, "Girl, you got this. Just take the first step." (Or picture Brené saying it. I won't be offended.)

Dear Inner Child,

Gosh, I used to be so ashamed of you. You were the part of me that I did everything to cover up. I learned to perform and be what others wanted, pushing down the things I didn't want people to see about you. The truth is, I've hidden you for so long because I was afraid of what people might think if they knew who I "used to be."

But now, I finally found the courage to sort through the layers that previously covered you in terrible shame. I've begun to see things more clearly. You felt like you had to perform to be seen and loved. You acted out and had terrible temper tantrums and tried to control people, all because you just wanted someone, anyone, to see you. I tried to reject you, believing I could walk away from who you are—but now I see that you've always been a part of me. As I've rejected you, I've also painfully rejected myself.

I'm sorry, my love. I'm sorry you felt like you had something to prove. I'm sorry you were drowning under the lies of too much and never enough. And worst of all, I'm sorry I rejected you after you felt rejected by everyone else. That must have been the most painful of all.

But guess what? All that ends now. With a heart full of compassion, I know that the only way to fix this is to move toward you. To prioritize connection with you. So, let's go on those Disney trips. Let's color creatively. Let's meditate together. Let's read fun and interesting stories of adventure and love. I'm ready for what you have to show me.

Thank you for the way you feel. Thank you for being expressive. Thank you for being creative. Thank you for your fiery passion.

Thank you for showing me that all of me is good and created by God.

You are part of me. I embrace you, and I love you.

Yours Truly,
Kait

Remember These Things

> You can't truly talk about rejection without facing the biggest way you self-reject: through your own self-hate.

> It can hurt like heck to dive into the depths of your past, face the reasons you've learned to hate yourself, and find a way to heal, but it can also destroy us a whole lot more to hold on and never let go.

> Your inner child is the part of yourself standing in the white room covered up by shame scarves. It's the part of you that you may have lost, hidden, or forgotten through time but that still resides in your subconscious.

> Fighting self-hatred and finding self-love are anything but linear. You never "arrive" at some perfect, ever-sustaining level of self-compassion. It's not a destination; it's a journey. Don't give up on the journey. Don't give up on the totality of who you are.

Ask These Things

> What is an early painful moment that caused you to dislike yourself? How does your adult self feel about this situation now? How did your inner child feel about this situation when it was happening?

> What is keeping you from facing what you don't like about yourself? If you have any numbing vices, what are they?

> How can you take steps to have compassion for your inner child?

Do These Things

> Reflect on the layers of shame scarves in your life. Start with the most difficult memories you endured in childhood and gradually work your way up.

> Develop a plan of action and rhythms to consistently connect to the deepest parts of your soul.

> Consider working through the painful parts of your past with a therapist. Nothing has helped me more than getting help from a trained professional.

> Write a thank-you letter to your inner child.

CHAPTER 3

Never Have I Ever

Fighting Sexual Shame

> The purity message is not about sex. Rather, it is about *us*: who we are, who we are expected to be, and who it is said we will become if we fail to meet those expectations. This is the language of shame.
>
> Linda Kay Klein

I fell in love for the first time at the age of fifteen. I met Ryan through a youth group Bible study I was a part of in high school. The year prior, I had transitioned from Catholicism to the evangelical world.

I'll never forget when Ryan asked me to officially be his girlfriend. It was on New Year's Day (sweet, right?). He surprised me with an adorable picnic, including a delicious array of food and desserts, that we spread out on the lawn of a local park filled with walking trails. Cue all the romance feels (*swoon*).

As the sun was setting, we kissed, which turned into making out, which progressed into heavier making out and cuddling together under a pile of blankets.

At that point in my teenage life, I had resolved that I was going to wait until marriage to have sex. But it turns out that keeping this promise when you're a sappy romantic and falling in love with a kind, loving, and empathetic guy who's sweeping you off your feet with grand romantic gestures is a lot harder than I had imagined.

Alas, back to the make-out sesh.

There we were—so enthralled with each other, that before we knew it, the sun set had set and the stars were out. The romantic allure of the twinkling stars and the cooler temperatures drew me even closer to Ryan.

Our making out progressed from sweet to passionate to ultra-steamy. Questions began swirling in my mind: *Why does this feel so different? Is this okay? Should I be ashamed of what I am feeling or what we are doing? Will God reject me because of this? Will the church reject me?*

We didn't have sex that night, but I went home feeling confused about whether our actions were okay and uncertain if how I felt was "bad" or not.

Shortly after that, two of our friends from the Bible study outed us by telling one of our group leaders that we had decided to become boyfriend and girlfriend without checking in with our community first—*whoops, thought we could make our own decisions, but apparently not.* Without hesitation, the leader arranged a meeting with both of us so he could talk through the process of "courting."

I'll never forget what came next.

The leader told us, "We don't encourage dating in our community unless both parties agree to prepare for marriage. Also, we only allow dating in groups. And lastly, here's a pledge of rules you must follow if you want to date."

I was then handed a piece of paper with a slew of rules that included things like the following:

- I agree not to sit next to the other party unless two pillows are between us at all times.
- I agree to keep our faces at least twelve inches apart at all times.
- I agree not to use any blankets.
- I agree not to kiss and to hold hands only on occasion.
- I agree never to be alone with the other party.
- I agree to "date" in group settings.

We were also pressured to meet with the group leader about every two weeks and begin premarital counseling. Did I mention we were mere teenagers? Sheesh (thanks a lot, *I Kissed Dating Goodbye*).[1]

In that moment, my spirit was torn. I felt conflicted both about what Ryan and I had already done physically and about whether I actually wanted to agree to all these rules and regulations.

But if I didn't agree to them, would we be judged by everyone around us? Would that mean the church was going to vote us off the island, and we'd be excommunicated forever? Would that mean God would be disappointed in me? Would I be *rejected?*

And what if they found out about what we had already done physically? Would we have to get on our knees and pray nonstop to repent from our actions? Was someone going to explain to us how we were now sexually broken and tainted forevermore?

I felt terrified of the consequences of my actions. I felt small and alone. I felt dirty and ashamed.

I want to pause the story here because I have a feeling this might be bringing up a few things for you too, especially one particular emotion: shame. And more specifically: sexual shame.

Thanks a Lot, Josh Harris

To be fair, we actually do talk about sex in the church, just not always in healthy and productive ways.

It shows up in shaming purity culture messaging. It shows up in the dialogue (albeit oftentimes unhealthy) with our Christian parents at the first sign of hormonal changes. It shows up in our youth groups and at purity ring gatherings. Whether or not we want to admit it, unhealthy dialogue related to sex has in many ways infiltrated the church.

To me, what has been the most damaging about these conversations, sermons, and practices is the soul-eating sexual shaming messages that have surfaced along the way, particularly as a way of controlling women.

Now, let me be clear: this is not limited to the church. We don't have to be brain scientists to know that outside the church, our culture is very much driven by sex. We are currently living in the midst of a real and, unfortunately, thriving hookup culture.

The book *Divine Sex* by Jonathan Grant reveals some staggering stats on sex and the church, one being that 69 percent of single Christian evangelicals say they have had sex with at least one person in the last year.[2] Does that sink in for you? That's right, 69 percent of single Christians who have been taught to abstain from sex are still having sex.

While the church may offer a plethora of purity teachings, there's clearly a gap between what evangelicals are taught and what they are actually doing when it comes to sex.

My relationship with Ryan is proof of this. Believe me, I had heard all the purity teachings. We were encouraged to adhere to specific rules and regulations. And yet, four months after we starting "dating in groups," a night came where we pushed the envelope. That particular evening, we managed to sneak away from the others. Our make-out session turned into our exploring each other's bodies, which turned into—you guessed it—having sex. I remember being internally conflicted the entire time, yet I didn't feel a strong enough pull to stop what was going on. I wanted to be physically intimate in that way, but I also didn't want to cross those lines. Momentary thoughts of how the community would reject me flashed through my mind, but in the heat of the moment, I was torn because he was someone I thought I loved. It felt wrong and right all at the same time. It was clear that what I was being told to believe and what I believed in the moment did not align.

Hello, hot mess of confusion!

After we had sex, my body felt like it was on a roller coaster of emotions—my stomach seized with tension and frustration. I was nauseated, on the verge of throwing up at a moment's notice. I remember collapsing into Ryan's arms, tears streaming down my face.

I told him I wasn't mad at him; I was mad at myself. I told him I was afraid of what God thought about what we had just done. I told him I was afraid of what other people would do if they found out. As I shared these feelings, I could feel a dark cloud of shame and the overwhelming fear of rejection encroaching.

Rejection of myself. *How in the world could I have let this happen?*

Rejection from others. *How appalled will they be to hear that we "fell into temptation"?*

Rejection from the church. *Will I even be allowed to step through the doors again without being shamed?*

Rejection from God. *Am I less of a Christian because I did this?*

The next day I woke up with a plan. I met Ryan in a coffee shop and pulled him to a table tucked in a corner.

"I know what we are going to do to make this right," I said to him. He stared back at me with a look of confusion tinged with fear.

I pulled my copy of *Every Young Woman's Battle* out of my bag. Before I left the house, I had snuck into my brother's room and grabbed his copy of the male version, *Every Young Man's Battle*. My mom had gifted us these books to help us on our abstinence journey. Honestly, I rolled my eyes when my mom first gave me the book, but now seemed like a better time than ever to crack it open.

"Alright," I said, looking at him with determination, "because of last night, we have to make sure we don't ever do this again. It's wrong. We both know it, and we have to be better. Okay?"

He nodded, prompting me to continue. "So, I think we should sit right here, read these books, and not leave until we know exactly where we failed and how we can do better next time."

Ryan looked at me with tears in his eyes and uttered, "Kait, I'm so sorry I let this happen." Gosh, the poor guy was taking all the responsibility on himself, likely feeling as though he had not been "man enough" to stop his sexual urges. This is a typical yet arguably unhealthy pressure put on men when it comes to sex that, in my opinion, is incredibly reductive.

Ryan agreed to my plan, so we sat there reading those two books, letting the words sink in. I sat directly across the table from him just to ensure we kept enough distance (had to leave room for the Holy Spirit, right?).

I think, in many ways, we both were terrified.

Throughout her book *Pure*, Linda Kay Klein talks about two competing ends of the purity binary. The process in which the evangelical church has introduced the purity concept to many adolescents has subtly (or, in some cases, not so subtly) encouraged two polarized sides. We are closer to God if we remain abstinent and "keep our purity," and we are further from God if we engage in any sexual activity, even merely the thought of anything sexual.[3]

Linda says, "The purity message is not about sex. Rather, it is about us: who we are, who we are expected to be, and who it is said we will become if we fail to meet those expectations. This is the language of shame."[4]

Any kind of messaging that shames us into a certain pre-scribed form of action is wrong. Any kind of community that seeks to make people seem "less than" if they mess up in any ca-pacity is lacking true love, compassion, mercy, and kindness—all staples of Jesus's character. And any church leadership that talks about sex as though it is in-herently wrong is not preaching true biblical doctrine.

Although I ended up "acting on fleshly desires" with Ryan, on the other end of the spectrum are people who heard purity culture messaging but did not have sex. Those individuals are still very much susceptible to the negative side effects of unhealthy messag-ing. The option for them was very often to repress their sexual de-sire, leaving them feeling distant and far removed from a very crucial part of their being. This suppression has been shown to have major effects on a person's ability to fully and freely connect with themselves as well as to connect one day with their spouse. This means that even people who have stuck to the rules of the purity culture have also suf-fered from toxic side effects.

> Any kind of community that seeks to make people seem "less than" if they mess up in any capacity is lacking true love, compassion, mercy, and kindness—all staples of Jesus's character.

If you could take a guess right now, what do you think hap-pened to Ryan and me in the wake of reading those two books (we were only teenagers at the time, might I remind you)?

Well, without feeling safe to tell anyone around us, we kept the secret between us. We hid it—stuffed it down, hoping and praying that by reading enough, all our temptations and guilt would go away.

But reading those books was just a temporary fix. The shame was too overwhelming to break through on our own. Slowly, over time, it ate away at us like a disease. As Carl Jung is reported to have said, "Shame is a soul-eating emotion." I don't just believe that; I lived it.

The reality is, when we live in shame about our sexual desire (or anything, for that matter), we become blocked from growing. When we don't feel as though we can share our stories or the intricacies of what's going on in our minds and hearts, we get lost. We need someone safe to share with. We need permission to reveal in confidence the things we are afraid to admit, knowing we will be met with empathy rather than judgment.

Brené Brown says, "If we can share our story with someone who responds with empathy and understanding, shame can't survive."[5]

Ryan and I were so pressured by purity teachings, how could we possibly have gone to our Bible group leader and told him what we had done? It's likely we would've been met with all the ways we had broken the rules of our said "contract," plunging us even deeper into the pool of shame.

And because of what our close Christian friends had also been taught about sexual purity, how could we go to any of them? They were taught the same doctrine; wouldn't they be just as judgmental?

I anticipated their responses . . .

"Kait, you *should have* stopped him."

"Kait, you *should have* had stricter boundaries."

"Kait, you *should have* put yourself in a less tempting situation."

"Kait, you *should have* been stronger."

You should have, you should have, you should have. Shame, shame, shame.

What I've learned about all this is that it isn't fair to be shamed into a way of believing. That's what "should-ing" does. It makes you adhere to specific rules that are enforced by fear rather than by love. The great part that people fail to mention? We have the power to stop letting people *should* on us.

> That's what "should-ing" does. It makes you adhere to specific rules that are enforced by fear rather than by love.

Deep-Seated Shame

Research has shown that participating in abstinence education and being sexually active = more sexual guilt. Also, sexual guilt from any first sexual interaction is predictive of higher sexual anxiety and lower sexual satisfaction.[6] And it's also most likely that girls will experience the majority of sexual guilt. While I don't believe that all purity teachings have bad motives, I do think they often have damaging undertones and are delivered poorly in ways that force men and women into deep-seated pits of shame.

My story also aligns with the research. Because I was ashamed of my sexual desire, and because I hid the sexual nature of my relationship with Ryan from everyone for the entirety of our relationship, a very deep and very real seed of blame was planted within me. And just like any seed, the shame-filled waters continued to nourish that seed as it began to grow a destructive and powerful root, eliminating my ability to see my sexual desire as good. This root of shame showed up in a variety of ways. It led me to consistently question my appearance around men. It made me feel uncomfortable about my body. It made me blame myself any time I ended up going "too far" with a guy. And it made me too afraid to talk about it whenever I did.

And then something else happened.

A few years ago, a friend asked me a question that I had never been asked before: "Have you ever been raped?" This question stopped me in my tracks. I felt my palms begin to sweat as thoughts of past events that I had pushed down for years came creeping back into my memory. I started to respond but hesitated. Finally, I let out a defeated, "I-I-I don't know."

Flashes of a past horrific evening with a well-known friend came to mind. Memories of a night I never wanted to revisit began to replay nonstop like a haunting movie in my head.

I sat next to the friend who had posed the question of whether I had been raped, completely stunned at the raw truth and confusion in my own response. I began thinking, *Wait, what? How could I not know if I was raped?*

I felt puzzled, fearful, angry, and sad all at once. What *really* happened all those years ago?

I think in my heart of hearts, I knew the truth. But because of all the messaging I had received throughout my formative years, it was difficult to see. At the forefront of my mind, all I could think of was this main message: "Make sure to never make your fellow brothers stumble," indicating that it's a woman's job to mitigate all lust. And since a man had made an advance on me, I clearly hadn't done a good enough job of that. This toxic message coupled with feeling a lack of safety to share my sexual past with just about anyone in my life led me to compartmentalize the events of this traumatic evening. I suffered from the same reasoning so many others experience: *I had been drinking. It must not count if I knew him. It was probably my fault anyway. I should have been more responsible to not tempt him.*

The full details of that horrific evening remain incredibly blurry, but here's what my memory can recall.

I was hanging out, seeking solace and comfort from a guy friend about a hard situation I was dealing with. He had a girlfriend who I was friends with, and he was a safe person for me—so I thought. Throughout the evening, he kept bringing me drink after drink, which I resolved to think was a nice gesture to help me cope. He offered to take me home, which then turned into him making a move on me. I remember telling him I was not comfortable and didn't want it. He replied with a version of "Just go with it, it's going to be fine." I didn't really know what was going on. I thought maybe allowing him to kiss me would satisfy his need and he'd be on his way. Nope. It continued. Silent tears rolled down my face as I lay there, feeling paralyzed during the act. A toxic combination of regret, sadness, fear, and worthlessness swirled around in my head, screaming, *Why is this happening? Is this what every man wants? Are all men unsafe? How could I let this happen? When is it going to end?* Afterward, I searched for my phone, only to realize he had taken it. I couldn't have called anyone even if I had wanted to . . . I felt trapped and overwhelmed with shame.

The next morning, I woke up feeling like I'd been bathing in a bucket of polluted water. He had cheated on his girlfriend with *me*, and all I could think about was that I let it happen. I was to blame. I began thinking, *Maybe he only did this because he felt bad for me. Maybe he was just trying to make me feel better. I could have stopped it if I wanted to.* The lies were eating me alive. Pieces of my heart were shattering as my insides felt like they were imploding. I didn't know what to do, who to tell, or what my next steps should be. I just wanted to hide it and pretend none of it had ever happened.

Which is what I did.

It wasn't until years later when my friend asked me if I'd ever been raped that I was forced to face the painful flood of emotions, memories, and sexual shame that I'd pushed down for years.

What makes me so sad about all this is that I had been conditioned to blame myself for any minor temptation, any misleading thought, or any sexual act I participated in. I had also been trained that if a man stumbles, it could very well be because I had been tempting him. Because of all this, I didn't feel safe sharing the incident with anyone, which could have been the key to helping me heal. Deep down, I felt responsible for what had happened—so much so that I pushed it down for years and years until one day I finally had the courage to open up about it.

Years later, I distinctly remember the day I decided to share my story online. The layers of fears kept slithering their way into my brain, trying to cripple me from pressing the publish button on my blog. *You cannot share this story, Kait. People will read it and say it wasn't sexual assault. They will think you are being dramatic.* I shudder today thinking that I, a woman who had been so unfairly taken advantage of, could have even had these fears. The multitude of years compounded with the plethora of lies had built up in my head until they were so overwhelming and in my face that I had mistaken them for truth. I blamed myself, thinking I was out of control, young, and reckless, and I should have known better.

Whether from shaming Christian messaging, cultural influences, family upbringing, or some toxic combination of all three, this is what so many of us get stuck doing in the wake of sexual assault: we blame ourselves. We think that because we knew the man or because we were tipsy or because of what we were wearing or just because we are a woman, that it is completely *our* fault that a man violated us. But, sister, can today be the day we put a stake in the ground saying that this heartbreaking, convoluted shaming and blaming messaging is no longer welcome?

If you are experiencing similar thoughts about your relationship with your own sexual experiences, or if you are painfully remembering a sexual assault, I am so very sorry. The pain and shame from such experiences are not your fault. We need support, we need to feel seen, we need healing, and we need to know we are not alone.

You are no less worthy because you were brutally taken advantage of.

Your sexual desire is not tainted.

God is not mad at you and in no way blames you.

In fact, no one has the right to blame you.

You were not irresponsible, naive, or at fault.

The clothing you wore doesn't mean you gave consent.

This was not your fault.

From the bottom of my heart, I need you to know you did not deserve what happened to you.

Hot tears stream down my cheeks as I write these words, because I know it still might be incredibly hard for you to receive them in the tender places of your precious heart and mind as truth. The self-blame and soul-eating shame might run so painfully deep that it may not be enough to hear the truth to make you fight through and rediscover the beauty of yourself, your body, and your sexual desire. I don't want to diminish the reality of this for you. But what I do know is this: on the other side of healing from our sexual rejection and past abuse lies the reclaiming of ourselves and our bodies.

Healing Our Sexual Wounds

I don't know about you, but when something starts boiling in me, I become eager to find a new way to fight for myself. But before we do that, we have to identify just exactly who and what we are dealing with.

The who is Satan. (Also known as the worst thing that ever happened to humanity. And can we all mutually agree that the name Satan just sounds like straight-up grossness?) He's an evil enemy whose only motive is to steal, kill, and destroy: steal our pride, kill our sense of love, and destroy our self-worth. And in its place, he wants to plant shame (that's the what), confounding our entire identity.

Just like any rebellious mastermind, he has a devious plan that he's had quite a long time to refine. His main trick has been to find and attack the areas that seem the most vulnerable to corruption in humans, like our sexual desire.

Satan has been lurking and preying in this area forever, adding layer of shame on top of layer of shame until we are so confused, we begin to hate our bodies and our sexual desire.

Shame acts like a barrier to keep love from getting through to our hearts. Shame says that our sexual desire is bad. Shame keeps people from being real about their struggles and their stories. Shame can be crippling in every area of our lives, but it can become especially life-sucking when it comes to our relationship with sex.

Let me be crystal clear: it's not our sexual desire that is inherently shameful but the *abuse* of our sexual desire that causes shame, and Satan is the primary culprit.

· The good news about all this? A man named Jesus.

Jesus was sent here to heal us completely and show us full unconditional love—a love so great, it wipes away every horrible thing that's ever happened to us. You've likely read countless stories of Jesus healing lepers, the lame, and the blind, not to mention becoming besties with the outcasts in society. Can we stop and process that for a second? The very people who were shamed and excluded by their community—Jesus healed them, was kind to them, and welcomed them in.

But here's what often happens. We read these stories of Jesus and think about how miraculous and kind and loving and wonderful and patient and forgiving he was—to everyone *else*.

But when it comes to ourselves, often stupid Satan has his grips so tightly wound around us (especially in how we view our sexual desire) that we become blind to the realization that this kind of healing and compassion is available for us too—through Jesus.

I get why you might feel confused about things that have happened to you or messages you've received from the church, culture, friends and family, and whomever else, but where is Jesus in all this? Why do we assume that he would reject us based on our sexual desire or past sexual experiences? His character consistently shows the opposite throughout the Bible, so why do we assume it would be different for us?

This is the first step to healing our sexual wounds. We need to bring the darkness into the light to finally expose for ourselves the revelatory truth about Jesus's loving character and God's heart for us.

The ways in which our sexual shame keeps us small, hidden, and in a cycle of self-blaming are countless, and if you're sick and tired (like I am) of being confused about the beauty of your own sexual desire, what do you say we work through this together? Because I promise you that there's another way. I promise you there's a way to get untangled from the web of confusion you find yourself in. And I promise you have it within you to take the journey. But I must warn you, it's not going to be easy. Because of that, I'm going to need you to reach into that bucket of grace and courage and splash yourself with some of that goodness, okay?

First, let's get a lay of the land to see what we are dealing with here. Start by asking yourself the following:

- How do I define sex?
- Have I ever thought of sex or my sexual desire as inherently bad?
- Have I ever been ashamed to share about my sexual urges or sexual actions with others?

- Have I ever felt like I had to follow certain protocols (even ones I didn't necessarily agree with) because church leaders told me to?
- Have I blamed myself for consensual sexual encounters?
- Have I blamed myself for nonconsensual sexual encounters?
- Have I ever felt the pressure to maintain "pure" for men?
- Do I believe that I have been negatively affected by purity culture?

Welp! You can't say I didn't warn you that we were going to get deep.

Maybe in processing these questions you're realizing your rejection of your own sexual desire has come from influences around you, such as your family, your friends, and even the church. While I don't necessarily believe anyone had the intention to shame you, keep you small, or force you into some fear-based way of thinking or acting, I also don't believe it was a fair situation.

For clarity purposes, I'm *not* saying we should completely forgo guidelines around sexual activity and have a free-for-all. Rather, I'm offering a way out of sexual shame and into holistic, biblical, grounded truths about sex and our sexual desires. I promise you, the freedom you'll find on this journey is unlike anything you've ever known.

To do this, we must break down the layers, analyzing them one by one, and work to rewrite the words, influences (church or otherwise), and situations that have sought to distort, damage, or shame our God-given sexual desire. In doing that, we will be able to renew and reestablish the core truths about our sexual desire and build a new truth grounded in love and clarity.

In order to get there, we must completely unravel our current belief system. We must take out all the pieces, lay them on the ground, and get real about analyzing each one.

First step? We have to break down the definition of sexual desire we've come to believe through the years so that we can align with this truth: God designed sex and said that it was good. In coming back to that truth, we must be incredibly introspective as we do our best to take this head knowledge and transform it into heart knowledge.

So, first, in breaking down your definition of sexual desire, I urge you to ask these questions about your beliefs:

- What do I believe God says about sexual desire?
- What do I believe about myself when it comes to my sexual desire?
- What do I believe about sexual desire overall (and what influences have shaped that belief)?

Was that eye-opening? Good. It should be.

Now that we've had a moment to look at our belief system, we can analyze each part of what makes up that belief system and ask *why* we have come to believe these things. Ask yourself these questions:

- What influences what I believe God says about sexual desire?
- What influences what I believe about my own sexual desire?
- What influences have shaped my overall beliefs about sexual desire?

Got that? Don't forget to dip into your bucket of grace and courage, okay?

Now, let's go one layer deeper.

It's time to discover a healthy and lasting meaning for sex and our sexual desire (I like to call this "forming a new sexual ethic") that is rooted in an understanding of both the beauty and sacredness of sex.

To go into this layer, ask yourself:

- Is there biblical evidence contrary to my beliefs about sexual desire?
- Am I attempting to interpret my beliefs about sexual desire without all the evidence?
- What would a mentor or someone I trust think about my belief system?
- If I try to look at sexual desire through a different lens, how does it impact my perspective?
- What does God want me to truly believe about my sexual desire?
- What do I want to truly believe about my sexual desire?

The last and final step in this process is accountability. Surround yourself with people who support and uphold you to the standard of belief you've communicated. Establish disciplines of obedience that align with this value system. If we aren't careful, the voices around us, coupled with the things we allow ourselves to see or do, just might infiltrate our system again. We have the *choice* to involve ourselves in communities filled with people who support and affirm the truth of God's message that's based on love and not fear. We *can* establish a sense of obedience that comes from a beautiful and deeply rooted understanding of our sexual desire, free of shame.

Here's the kicker: the process of questioning and breaking down these beliefs to craft a new, healthy, beautifully holistic view of sex and our sexual desire that's rooted in truth cannot (and should not) be done in the blink of an eye.

It's taken me years to rewrite the shame I endured through the teachings of the purity culture and the "I Kissed Dating Goodbye" movement. It's also taken a timely process to heal from the sexual abuse I endured.

It's taken even longer to truly develop disciplines and practices that feel in line with my values. And believe me, it is still very much a journey.

> We can establish a sense of obedience that comes from a beautiful and deeply rooted understanding of our sexual desire, free of shame.

I love talking about this with my dear friend Kat Harris. She's a thirty-five-year-old virgin in NYC, living out her best "sexless in the city" life, if you will. Kat is very open about her journey of saving sex until marriage. She talks about a time years ago that she dated a man she had an incredible connection with. She had resolved to wait to have sex until marriage, but in the throes of passion, she found it incredibly difficult to actually *want* to uphold her values and abstain.

She openly shares that she ended up crossing boundaries she had set for herself, minus the actual act of intercourse. However, this experience led her on a journey of questioning why she was even being so strict about this value in the first place. What influences impacted what she really believed about sex? What did God say about sex? Why was she truly choosing to abstain? Was it all even worth it?

Kat's journey led her down a yearlong path of talking to pastors, friends, and psychologists and diving deep into books, podcasts, and research. She even looked up every verse in the Bible that talks about sex. She expected to come out of that year of searching convinced that she should just break the ice and "do the deed," aka finally have sex.

But after 365 days of soul-searching, researching, breaking down the layers, and prayerfully questioning all these things with God, she came out with more clarity and more boundaries than she'd had before. She had done the work of debunking and healing the shame that lived within her. She began fully understanding what she actually believed about sex. She started to truly comprehend what God said about sex. And, most importantly, she finally understood her *why*.

Today, I encourage you to do whatever you can to discover the beauty of your sexual desire as it was originally designed by God. Tap into the endless love and compassion available through Jesus. Do whatever it takes to heal from your past sexual shame and begin moving into newfound freedom. Spend time breaking down the layers so you can understand how you got here and begin to rewrite what this all means to you. And in this process, discover and define your deep and true why, a why that will strengthen you, empower you, free you, enlighten you, and newly define you.

Your sexual desire is good. You were made for good things, purposed by God.

Your sexual desire is good. You were made for good things, purposed by God. It's time to eradicate the shame and reclaim this for yourself.

Dear Sexual Desire,

I used to be ashamed of you, and in ways, afraid of you. I didn't understand why I felt certain things, and though you are an inherent part of me, I didn't feel as though I could embrace you, because I was constantly told you were sinful. Rules, regulations, a lack of true understanding—all of it made me hide you, shame you, keep you small with the sole goal of trying to contain you.

Today I want to thank you. Thank you for making me feel, thank you for helping me connect, and thank you for being an inherent and good part of who I am. I'm sorry for rejecting you for so long, and I'm sorry for the ways in which I allowed other people's influence to make me reject you as well. Now that I understand you more, I'm allowing myself to feel, to move, to love, to live more freely. And because of that, I have deeper gratitude for how you are a part of me.

From now on I choose to honor you, respect you, love you, and embrace you. You are a beautiful part of how God uniquely wired me. (Oh, and about sex? I cannot wait to experience that safely and beautifully in the covenant of marriage one day.)

Yours Truly,
Kait

Remember These Things

> - It's true that 69 percent of single Christian evangelicals say they have had sex with at least one person in the last year. While the church may have a plethora of purity teachings, there's clearly a gap between what evangelicals are taught and what they are actually doing when it comes to sex.

> - Any kind of messaging that shames you into a certain pre-scribed form of action is wrong. Shame acts like a barrier to

keep love from getting through to your heart. Shame is a soul-eating emotion.

> In the first step to healing your sexual wounds, you need to bring the darkness into the light to finally expose the revelatory truth about Jesus's loving character and God's heart for you.

> You can establish a sense of obedience that comes from a beautiful and deeply rooted understanding of your sexual desire, free of shame.

Ask These Things

> How has it felt when people "should" on you? How are you going to fight for yourself and stop that?

> How has your sexual shame kept you trapped?

> Who are you surrounding yourself with, how have they affected you, and how can you keep accountable to a healthier dialogue about sex and sexual desire?

Do These Things

> Reflect on all the questions in the chapter regarding your belief system.

> Write your new sexual ethic.

> Write a thank-you letter to your sexual desire.

CHAPTER 4

Sorry, Not Sorry

Fighting Not Fitting In

True belonging doesn't require you to *change* who you are; it requires you to *be* who you are.

Brené Brown

When I was seven, I was the little girl wearing dresses and climbing trees. I wanted to be adventurous and cute at the same time (can you blame me?). In middle school, I started secretly raiding my mother's closet and borrowing her scarves, headbands, and purses. I remember getting on the school bus, and as soon as it turned the corner away from home, I'd think, *Coast is clear!* Cue the classic nineties makeup routine (i.e., lots of blue eyeshadow). My Caboodles kit felt like my own personal paint set: the options for hair and makeup were endless. I couldn't understand why others would make fun of me for wanting to be my very own Claude Monet. Didn't they appreciate that waking up at 5:00 a.m. to do my hair a different way every day in the fifth grade took a ton of creativity?

In sixth grade, a good friend of mine, Suzy, decided to morph into Regina George from the movie *Mean Girls*. She began spreading lies about me to all my closest friends, and as naive eleven-year-olds, they, of course, believed her. Suzy successfully had her army of mean girls.

They began leaving mocking notes in my locker written in pastel gel pens. When they saw me walking toward them, they'd run to the nearest wall and make grotesque sounds as if I smelled. They stopped inviting me to friend gatherings and birthday parties and sleepovers (the thing every eleven-year-old lives for). They refused to let me sit with them at lunch. Eventually, I befriended the only other girl in our grade who also looked alone, Mindy.

I didn't really understand it at the time, but now I realize how painfully misunderstood I felt.

Being misunderstood wreaks havoc on our core human needs: to be seen, heard, and loved as we are. I didn't see anything wrong with my passion for fashion or my desire to be a teacher's pet, but because it wasn't tailored to what everyone else thought was acceptable, or maybe even because others were even jealous, I was shunned, judged, teased, and ultimately bullied.

Being misunderstood can be painfully isolating. It can feel like you've been hit with a viral plague that everyone wants to flee from—à la COVID-19. As the pressure to feel accepted heightens, instead of holding tighter to what makes you unique, you begin to resent it. You wish it would disappear as you become desperate to do anything to just simply belong.

As much as I loved fashion and beauty, the pain and loneliness of being an outsider were too isolating to bear, and I certainly didn't want to go into the seventh grade being bullied. I decided to take a page out of Cady's book from *Mean Girls* when she tried to gain entry into the Plastics; I resolved to act like everyone else in order to be accepted by them (even if that meant being everything but myself).

I remember buying those three-stripe Adidas shoes, wearing my hair the "plain jane" way (RIP to all my funky hairstyles!), and getting an L.L.Bean backpack all to feel like I was one of *them*. I tried to apologize to Suzy—though I wasn't even sure what I was apologizing for—and attempted to flood her with niceties.

This is what the pains of feeling misunderstood can do. We long for even a small semblance of acceptance and often sacrifice who we are for the sake of being what others want us to be, and it's destroying us in the process. We might silence our voice for fear of judgment. We might change the way we dress or the way we look to conform to the status quo. We might sacrifice our love for the arts because everyone else says we should have a high-powered career instead. We might stop eating the foods we love so we can start looking like the skinniest girls around us.

The desire to belong and be understood manifests differently for all of us, but the inherent messaging boils down to one core concept. Being misunderstood sends a giant signal to our brains that screams, "You need to change to be accepted."

The hard part about feeling misunderstood and desperate to belong is that in some ways, we **are pretty helpless.** Despite all our efforts, we cannot force someone to see us and accept us. We have zero control over whether others receive us for who we are.

> Being misunderstood sends a giant signal to our brains that screams, "You need to change to be accepted."

But what if it doesn't matter what they think of us? What if it doesn't matter if people understand the things that make us different? What if the real power lies in being able to see and embrace that we are welcome just as we are?

Because isn't it true that God created us all to be different? And isn't it natural that there are things that make us, *us*? For instance, whether that's being an introvert or an extrovert. Preferring to visit a museum over going to a sports game. Jammin' to Lecrae or solely listening to oldies. Being perfectly neat and tidy or tolerating a little clutter. For me, being a girly girl is part of my personality. It's in the inherent DNA of how God created me. (And to clarify, I in no way think that just because you're a woman, you should want to be super girly. That's just the case for me.)

What if there were a way to truly see and embrace that we are welcome just as we are despite feeling misunderstood and rejected by others?

I believe there is, which leads me to ask the following:

- How do we find the courage to walk in self-acceptance in environments where people choose not to fight against their preconceived ideas or get out of their comfortable bubbles to learn more about us?
- How do we feel loved even when we don't feel as though we belong?
- Where do we really belong, and is it possible to find that place for ourselves?
- Along the way, how can we accept (and maybe even anticipate) the hard truth that sometimes we might be misunderstood?

Finding my own sense of belonging has been a lifelong trek for me, and I am still in the midst of it. But what I know for sure is that if we don't find a way to true belonging, the environments where people misunderstand us will crush our souls and potentially compromise our identities. I don't want that for you as much as I don't want it for me. I want you to know your inherent value and true worth regardless of whether others do.

And I'm positive that our amazing, loving, perfect Father (God in heaven) who crafted us just as we are wants that for us as well.

This is the journey to discovering our own true belonging.

Be Your People

Now, what does a girly girl who feels like she needs to change in order to belong do with her life? Well, in this case, she goes to merchandising school to become a fashion connoisseur, determined to live out her perfect Anna Wintour life. But really, in her heart of hearts, she's on a mission to find her people. *But of course.*

When you feel like you don't belong, finding your people seems essential to your survival. When you're constantly misunderstood, you'll do just about anything to find a place where you can feel accepted and loved for who you are. You might change jobs or move to a different city or try a new church or shift your entire friend group. You'll likely go to any length, big or small, to find people who finally get you.

After college and a few years into my fashion career, I landed my dream role: a buyer at Barneys New York. As Emily in *The Devil Wears Prada* would say, "A million girls would kill for your job."[1] Alas, I thought I had made it. Not only was this the career I had always dreamed of, but I also believed I had found an environment where people would fully embrace my style, my uniqueness, and my personality. *These people will get me,* I told myself. I figured I'd strut in there like Carrie Bradshaw and surely walk out with three new fashionable besties by the names of Samantha, Charlotte, and Miranda.

It all seemed totally plausible . . . in my head. It wasn't long before my dreams of gleaning a fashionista girl tribe would be shattered.

Feeling misunderstood by people who are totally different from you is one thing. Feeling like you don't belong with the people you *think* are your people is another. At Barneys and among the people I *thought* would grant me instant belonging, I still didn't find that intimate, true feeling that I really belonged.

Here's the hard lesson I learned: just because you land in a sea of people who seem like you doesn't mean you're automatically going to feel like you belong.

The tough part about belonging is that you can search and search and search and jump around from place to place as much as you want, but you'll be hard-pressed to find an environment where every person accepts you.

Even if you're the Mother Teresa of the modern decade, there's always going to be that one internet troll who finds a flaw in what you're doing or who you are. And here's the even harder truth: while you might feel like you are on a journey to belong, often what you're actually trying to do is fit in.

Let's see what the master Brené Brown says about fitting in, shall we?

My girl Brené (well, at least I'd like to think she's my girl) talks about belonging as one of our ultimate *core* needs as human beings. She also says that the opposite of belonging is "fitting in." Fitting in is instead assessing the scene and acclimating accordingly. It's about upholding a standard of what you think others need you to be. It's about thinking what you think you need to say or what you think you need to wear or what you need to look like or what job you need to have. And in the process of trying to fit in, you totally lose sight of the uniqueness that makes you perfectly you.

Fitting in is not belonging; it's abandoning our identity. It's forgoing the unique things that make us, *us*. It's rejecting how we were created for a fleeting, superficial like that will never last.

When I decided to limit myself to being around only people just like me, it wasn't actually helping me feel more like myself. Whether in middle school or in a work environment where people have similar passions, it didn't matter whether all those people understood me. I had yet to realize that looking for people like me to tell me I belonged would continue to leave me a little lost and very empty-handed.

> **Fitting in is not belonging; it's abandoning our identity. It's forgoing the unique things that make us, *us*. It's rejecting how we were created for the sake of being superficially liked.**

Be Who You Are

What I've come to learn is that no matter where we go or what job we obtain or how many accolades we acquire, it doesn't matter if everyone appears to be like us or no one is like us. At the end of the day, we can face unfamiliar crowds and still feel like we belong if we first and foremost find belonging within *ourselves*.

This is the ultimate way we can stay strong amid the environments that reject us. We must find ways to belong to ourselves. To stand by our convictions. To love the unique parts of our personalities. To embrace our little quirks. To walk without fear of whether others are going to accept us. To know we are loved even when others do not let us belong. When we finally step into owning our true worth, others don't have nearly as much power to knock us down with their rejection.

To walk this out, we must be our own people, our own dream team, our own advocates. No one on this planet can make us feel true belonging, unless we first accept ourselves. True belonging is about speaking our truth, upholding our values and convictions, and unashamedly refusing to change the things about us that make us unique and beautiful people. I love how Brené Brown says it:

> True belonging does not require you to *change* who you are; it requires you to *be* who you are.[2]

If we want to choose to accept ourselves fully as we are, and if we are doing our best to live holy, kind, and meaningful lives, then it doesn't exactly matter what the world says about us, does it?

> True belonging is about speaking our truth, upholding our values and convictions, and unashamedly not changing the things about us that make us unique and beautiful people.

If we are going to fight the fear of being misunderstood and not belonging, we have to do something a bit hard, okay? We have to learn to be okay with not being liked. It's going to take a whole lot of grit, self-control, and mental clarity. I know, it's hard, but I promise with every ounce of my being that it's worth it.

In order to accept not always being liked, we must find a way to come back to accepting ourselves just as we are, in alignment with how our precious God sees us.

If you constantly struggle with knowing who you are, how God sees you, and what you were created for, I'd love to offer some basic but helpful ways for you to break that down.

Step 1: Come Back to God's Truths

Coming back to ourselves doesn't have to involve an elaborate quest with bougie therapy, weekend retreats, or pricey self-help courses (though, trust me, I am all about that therapy life). The very best thing we can do is turn to the basic yet powerful truths that God lays out in his precious Word. Whenever I need a dose of remembering who I am and how I am uniquely designed, I read my go-to chapter in the Bible: Psalm 139. In the Passion Translation, this chapter is called "You Know All About Me." It's the perfect passage to make me feel deeply known. Getting lost in the verses "I am fearfully and wonderfully made" (v. 14) and "You knit me together in my mother's womb" (v. 13) gives me permission to accept who I am because I am reminded that God created me this way purposefully and uniquely. When I read Psalm 139, I usually say it out loud with passion and conviction in my voice, as though I'm reciting my very own powerful declaration of belonging. Go ahead and try it. Read it out loud to yourself (because I assure you, reading it out loud is utterly thrilling). Read it once slowly, then read it again passionately and highlight words that stand out to you. Read it as many more times as it takes for you to soak in the entirety of its meaning. I promise, these loving words and truths will never disappoint.

Step 2: Phone a Friend

Now it's time to think about the tangible, unique, and beautiful things you can offer the world. If you're not sure, then let's take a cue from the famous *Who Wants to Be a Millionaire?* idea of "phone a friend," shall we? It can be so easy to see the unique beauty in other people and not see it in ourselves. So, it's time to call your closest friends and ask them to reflect back to you the truths of what they see in you. Sometimes we need another set of eyes to help us clear our blind spots and truly see the unique gifts we bring to the world. Our friends can do that by mirroring to us what they see in us and have experienced by having us in their lives.

Guess what? Our friends actually don't have to be friends with us. Nope, they have a choice. And if they are choosing to be friends with us, they are making that decision for a reason. I'm going to go out on a limb here and say it's likely because we bring something special and life-giving to their lives—it's because they actually find something special about us.

Becoming crystal clear about the unique things you have to offer this world while also loving and accepting the fun, quirky, or different parts of your personality leads to a deeper calling to use these unique things to bless humanity around you. Over time, a fire starts building within your soul. A fire that says, *I know who I am and what I have to offer, and nothing will stop me from using these things to bless others however I can.*

When you start to walk with this fire in your soul, it becomes less scary when you come into contact with people who don't accept you as you are. If someone misunderstands you, you let it roll off your shoulder like a weightless raindrop, because you are firm in who you are and are not here to waste your time convincing people to see the things you know are true about yourself.

Oh, and while you're at it, if you want life-giving and affirming friendships, make sure you are serving out just as much sweet love and truth nectar to them as they're gifting to you.

Step 3: Stop Apologizing

A huge part of belonging to ourselves and accepting who we are means that we have to learn to stop apologizing for who we are. I'm going to be real with you, friend, that trying to *not* apologize . . . well, this has been the *bane* of my actual existence.

I am notorious for saying sorry for just about *everything*.

"Sorry, I'm talking so much."

"Sorry, I'm having a bad day."

"Sorry, I have so many feelings."

"Sorry, I look gross today."

"Sorry. Sorry. Sorry. Sorry."

But I think it's about time to put our Demi Lovato pants on and start living as though we are "sorry, *not* sorry."

Now, here's the caveat: if you're flat-out being rude, mean, inconsiderate, or selfish, then by all means, please apologize and seek to right your wrongs. When we do something to hurt someone or are not being very considerate of another or are only thinking selfishly, we should apologize and make it right. That's just human decency.

But that's not all I hear people apologizing for, and it sure isn't what I only say sorry about. More often than not, I apologize for just being myself when an apology is completely unnecessary. Every time I say these words, I am not accepting the whole of who I truly am.

Recently I realized this had to stop. I made a pact with myself and my small group at Onsite that I was going to stop apologizing for the woman I am. This came on the heels of my desire to impress a man who was breaking it off with me because I didn't wear Patagonia, drive a jeep, or go camping. The problem was that he wasn't the first guy who had been that specific in his so-called preferences. He was more like the fifth I-just-want-a-casual-chill-girl-who-goes-camping-all-the-time offender.

I was so fed up that I was tempted to say, with enough coercing, I could eventually learn to love wearing Patagonia, driving a jeep, and sleeping on the hard, flat ground while getting eaten alive by bugs all in the name of the great outdoors. But who am I kidding? That's not me. It's never been me and will never be me. (By the way, if you're a camping gal, that is so rad. By all means, please be you!)

My Onsite group helped remind me that I had spent years of my childhood and adult life trying to fit in, which led to a flood of self-questioning and trying to be everyone else but myself, eradicating my true value. It was time to put a stop to this behavior.

They made me repeat this to myself: "Kait, not one drop of your self-worth depends on his acceptance of you." I also started to realize what it looks like to unapologetically accept myself. Self-acceptance is not about apologizing when you aren't exactly who someone wants you to be. Like Christina Grimmie said, "Confidence is not 'they will like me.' Confidence instead is 'I'll be fine if they don't.'"[3] Stop for a second and reread that. How fabulous does that sound? Come on, now!

Right then and there, I chose to stop apologizing for not being outdoorsy enough. Maybe in your case, you need to stop apologizing for not doing your makeup like Kylie Jenner because you prefer a more natural look. Or maybe you need to stop apologizing for not having every Bible verse memorized to prove you have a deep relationship with God. What is it that drives you to say sorry to people for something that you shouldn't be sorry for in the first place?

One of my group members, Jessica, wrote *PATAGONIA*, *JEEPS*, and *CAMPING* in big block letters on three bright-yellow note cards. She showed me the cards, took a big black Sharpie, and drew a giant *X* on all three.

These note cards now act as the bookmarks in my daily journal. They speak a message that, honestly, I need to be reminded of daily. A message that tells me, "It's okay to be unashamedly who you are." And, my friend, it's time for you to also accept that truth for yourself. You have permission.

What are you apologizing for? What words would you write on your cue cards to cross out? What have you believed you need to change about yourself to be accepted?

Don't forget—not one drop of your self-worth depends on other people's acceptance of you.

> Don't forget—not one drop of your self-worth depends on other people's acceptance of you.

Be the Change You Want to See

Remember when I was being bullied in the sixth grade and befriended Mindy, who also felt incredibly alone that year? She was in the band with me, and we even shared some classes, but prior to this I hadn't noticed her.

I remember confiding about my experience to my sixth-grade health teacher that year, Mrs. Jones. When I learned

Mindy's story, I realized she had felt this way much longer than I had. My heart sank and ached. I could barely deal with this experience for the entirety of sixth grade. I couldn't imagine it swallowing me whole for years on end. I asked my teacher what I could do to help Mindy, and she simply said, "Kait, it's unfair, but everything can change with an act of kindness. Be the change you want to see."

So, I did. I welcomed her into my life as a friend, and she welcomed me into her life as a friend. Our friendship healed me in ways I didn't even know I needed.

Here's what I learned: sometimes simply saying, "Come sit with me" can be the greatest act of love.

It's like the legendary Maya Angelou said, "I learned a long time ago the wisest thing I can do is be on my own side, be an advocate for myself and others like me."[4]

If you've felt misunderstood, then chances are a gazillion other women feel just like you: alone, confused, unheard, afraid to really be themselves. As you go on this journey of truly seeing yourself as God sees you and walking in the value of who you really are, I want to also encourage you to gift this to others. Be the person who doesn't run away from someone who looks or acts totally different from you. Challenge yourself to show up in places other than the settings you are used to. Be on the lookout for the ones who want to feel seen and heard. They need your welcoming spirit. Break out of your bubble and experience the beauty that lies in the world of discomfort. You just might realize there's a whole lot more life to be found when you intentionally open your eyes toward others.

Really seeing and accepting others means going on a journey of curiosity. It means caring about why someone is different from you, taking steps to learn more about what makes that person who they are, and in the meantime being willing to have some tough conversations. Unless you are willing to get curious and maybe even a bit uncomfortable, you'll miss the chance to grow your perspective, meet people who truly challenge you, and even (on the most beautiful occasions) realize you aren't as different from them as you thought.

What if, in a sea of people who are constantly questioning whether they are seen, heard, or accepted, you become the one who starts gifting belonging to others? What if that small act provides someone with a little more sense of love for themselves? What if it helps them see themselves the way God actually sees them?

And for those who you strongly connect with, share your story and struggle of being on this journey—of battling being seen, heard, and accepted. You never know how your experience could be the catalyst for someone else to unlock a sense of connection and self-acceptance. You never know how sharing your own journey of fighting for and finding true belonging could help someone else heal.

I know we might not officially know each other in real life, but today I want to tell you that no matter how different or similar we may be, I'd be honored to learn more about you. And if given the chance, I'd love to hear your story. I'd get in my favorite cozies and soak in every word. Want to know why? Because you are always welcome at my table, you are always invited to my party. Your uniqueness is important because God made you uniquely perfect, just as you are.

Dear Fitting In,

Throughout the years, you've fed me messages like, "You need to change to be accepted," "This will make you better," "Your voice doesn't matter," and "You aren't like everyone else." Sometimes these thoughts have become as unbearably loud as a fire alarm ringing in my ears. They've tempted me to change everything about myself.

I've tried abandoning what I love, the things that make my soul dance with firey passion, but all it gave me in return was a hollow feeling of self-betrayal. Other times these thoughts have led me to hide or get quiet or flee until I found some sense of normalcy.

I've done everything I can to fight this messaging and find somewhere I feel wanted, desired, and free to be me.

But now, today, all that ends. I'm done trying to fit in, because fitting in means abandoning who I am for the sake of others. And even when everyone else seems like me, I still don't feel I fit in. No, what I want is true belonging. And that comes by intimately knowing my value like the back of my hand, wearing my uniqueness like a proud ensemble, and strutting confidently in shoes that show I accept the entirety of who I am.

True belonging requires me to just be me.

So, from here on out, I'm walking in my value, upholding my own convictions, and never, ever again changing the things about me that make me uniquely beautiful. Sometimes I won't be liked, and I'm okay with that now, because isn't that the risk of being human?

Now that I've found this freedom, I'm going to do my best to help others find the same. I'm committed to welcoming, inviting, including, and saying, "You are welcome here," for this really is the deepest kind of love.

Thank you for helping me see that. I'm thankful that I belong just because I am me.

Yours Truly,
Kait

Remember These Things

> Belonging is a core human need. Everyone wants to be seen, heard, and loved as they are. Fitting in is not belonging; it's abandoning your identity. It's forgoing the unique things that make you, you. It's rejecting how you were created for the sake of a fleeting, superficial like that will never last.

> The tough part about belonging is that you can search and search and search and jump around from place to place as much as you want, but you'll be hard-pressed to find an environment where every person accepts you.

> Not one drop of your self-worth depends on other people's acceptance of you. *You* can give yourself the gift of belonging by, first and foremost, learning to accept yourself as you are.

> What if, in a sea of people who are constantly questioning if they are seen, heard, or accepted, you become the one who starts gifting belonging to others?

Ask These Things

> Have you ever done things for the sake of "fitting in"?

> What have you believed you needed to change about yourself to be accepted?

> Who are you? How does God specifically see you? What were you created for?

> What are the things you're apologizing for? Name them.

Do These Things

➢ Phone a friend and ask them, "What unique things do you think I bring to this world? Why are you my friend?"

➢ Grab some note cards, write down the things you need to stop apologizing for, and cross them out. Put them where you can regularly see them.

➢ Look for someone in your life who may feel like they don't belong. Invite them out to coffee, over for a meal, or to the next group event you plan to attend. Get curious. Start being the change you want to see.

➢ Write a thank-you letter to fitting in.

CHAPTER 5

The Ugly Cry

Fighting Heartbreak

Within the valley of our grief, something beautiful wants to grow. Tend those fields, water those little seeds. What was planted in pain, can harvest beautiful possibilities.

Mike Foster

It was a Sunday afternoon in early August. I was lying on the bed, still in my pajamas because I was too tired to put on real clothes, incessantly replaying the events of the previous night. My boyfriend at the time, Chris, and I had had a fight—which was rare for us—and this one hadn't ended pretty.

I racked my brain trying to recall how in the world we'd ended up in such a downward spiral. I couldn't actually remember all the details, but I knew the fight had ended in tears, frustration, and Chris's leaving so neither one of us would say anything we regretted. Sadly, that hadn't stopped me from sending texts to him in my emotional spiral shortly after he left (I wish someone had been there to take my phone away—you feel me?).

The next morning, rereading through the late-night texts revealed more of the story. As I scrolled through the messages, I felt a mix of sadness and utter embarrassment. I had literally written the words *someone as solid as you shouldn't be dating a hot mess like me.* And then, the cherry on top: *you deserve better.* Yup, that was it. I wanted to crawl into a hole and hide forever.

Ever had that feeling?

Chris came over so we could talk about what happened the night before. I sat there staring at the man I thought without a shadow of a doubt I was going to marry. His dark hair, deep-brown eyes, and smile filled with love and compassion—this was someone I so deeply loved and would do anything for. Was this actually *happening?* Was this really *the end?*

As he opened his mouth to speak, everything moved in slow motion. "Kait," he said, "I don't know what it is, but I don't have peace about our relationship." In an instant, it felt like the walls were caving in around me and the windows were shattering. I could barely breathe.

It wasn't supposed to be this way. I wanted to remain in the fairy tale that had existed a mere twenty-four hours earlier. In my mind, we were the couple who was more in love than ever, prancing through fields of flowers toward our beautiful destination of marriage. I loved playing Scrabble by the ocean. I endured staying up late to have extra time with him because he was a night owl. When he spoke affirmations, it was as though his sincere and loving words cloaked my heart with gold. Our twenty-minute hugs with no talking felt like an exchange of a thousand loving words.

This was my *man . . .*

We were supposed to be together forever, and now suddenly, out of nowhere, the relationship with the very person I prayed for, loved, and desired so deeply was disappearing right before my eyes.

Oh, what I would have given for Will Smith to have popped onto the scene, pulled out his Neuralyzer, and eradicated every memory of this ever happening—*Men in Black* style.

This heartbreak crushed my soul into a million little pieces. Though it wasn't the first painful heartbreak I had ever endured, it felt unbearable.

I was terrified to face the questions looming in my mind: If this seemingly healthy and loving relationship didn't work, what did that mean for *my future*? What did that say *about me*?

How could I find any semblance of strength to get up again when I'd been hit down so many times? How could I find hope when I'd put so much time and effort into thinking this was it? And how could I move forward again when I'd already done the work to sort, comfort, and slowly bandage up my tattered heart from previous heartbreaks?

This was my biggest nightmare.

Why Does Heartbreak Hurt So Bad?

Have you ever felt the deep, soul-wrenching pain of a heartbreak? Could you feel the ache coursing through your body as though you were being fed an IV of toxic liquids? Have you physically felt sick, maybe even thrown up? Have you found yourself facedown, weeping on the floor, barely able to catch your breath?

After that conversation with Chris, I felt like someone could have wheeled me into a hospital. I imagine the conversation would have gone something like this:

"Hello, Kait. What's the problem?"

"Doc, the pain in my chest is so intense. My heart is broken, and I don't know if it's reparable this time."

Even to this day, years later, I can still recount the vivid details and feel the visceral pain hitting me square in the gut. The memories come flooding back, as do the tears.

A shattered heart can feel equivalent to a sudden (and unwarranted) explosion in not only your life but also your body. *Why* does heartbreak feel like physical pain inflicted on your body?

When you are feeling physical pain from heartache, it might be because your *sympathetic nervous system* (aka your fight-or-flight response) is activated at the same time as your *parasympathetic nervous system* (aka your rest-and-digest response). In this way, it's like you are pumping the gas and pressing the brakes at the same time, creating an actual sensation of heartbreak.

> A shattered heart can feel equivalent to a sudden (and unwarranted) explosion in not only your life but also your body.

A study at Rutgers University revealed that when thoughts of the heartbreaker came into the minds of the heartbreak-ee, sadness, anger, frustration, despair, confusion, or whatever other heartbreaking emotion they were feeling actually triggered the same sensation as physical pain in the subject's brain.[1]

Well, that certainly makes sense, doesn't it?

It gets worse. Right when you're down and weak, you come face-to-face with the lies about yourself, your goodness, and often your value.

While I was reeling from heartache, feeling the physical and emotional pain, I told myself something hurtful: "Kait, you are good but never enough."

There it is. The destructive yet incredibly convincing lie that has plagued me as a single woman. I cringe writing these words that have so deeply poisoned my mind for years (and I'm holding myself back from writing a few choice words in utter frustration). In the moment of receiving the shocking "I don't have peace" news from Chris, I felt this life-sucking belief resurfacing, trying to latch on to me like a leech coming for its feeding.

As Chris took a week of space to think about things before deciding on the ultimate fate of our relationship, I had my own decision to make. I wasn't convinced that I wanted to play the wounded victim stuck in the aftermath of a bombing. While the breakup was unexpected, didn't make sense, and hurt like no other (I'd rather have to endure waxing every day for the rest of my life than face this), I took a moment to breathe and recognized that though I was overwhelmed, I had power, and with that, options. As I racked my brain, I realized I could choose to do the following:

A. Stay small, weak, and wounded. Succumb to the pain, refuse to get up. Allow the lie of "good but never enough" to have its way with me like a flesh-eating disease.

OR

B. Go back to easy and unhealthy vices that feel good in the moment, such as the ever-so-alluring habit of scrolling on social media. Or drink a bottle of wine and binge the latest popular Netflix show. Or pour myself into my work in order to have as little time with my emotions as possible.

OR

C. Find a way within the ruins to fight my biggest lies of heartbreak. Tap into my bucket of adrenaline, stand back up, and do whatever I could to defend myself against the lies flying my way.

Sure, the sting of this reality had already done initial damage, but I had the *choice* to accept my biggest heartbreak lie as truth or believe something else.

Fighting Your Biggest Heartbreak Lies

The following weekend, I went to my favorite little park by the ocean to spend some quality time with God. I sat on my favorite blanket and placed a notebook, a pen, and my Bible in front of me. I took a moment to sit in my woundedness and let the pain seethe.

If I'm being honest, options A and B were looking as tempting as an In-N-Out Double-Double (protein style, of course). Part of me wanted to succumb to weakness, to let down my guard and allow the painful lies to have at it. But I knew that would be the cue to open the floodgates to fear and worthlessness. Like an unsteady domino, I would inevitably topple into dating someone else in an attempt to fill the massive void in my heart, leading me right back to where I started: contemplating my enoughness.

The other side of me wanted to discreetly flee the scene, pretending that none of these lies existed as I went into my usual mechanisms of distracting myself with work, busyness, and performance. I'd possibly start a side business, try extra hard at my day job, go to all the social events I possibly could, work out excessively, and binge *Grey's Anatomy* whenever I wanted (RIP, Denny Duquette), all while avoiding my emotions. But I also knew option B came with an expiration date that usually looked like an ugly meltdown driven by exhaustion and confusion.

While tempting, these choices had never ultimately served my heart in the past. I decided that if I was going to go with option C, I was going to have to feel the pain to heal the pain, which also meant I was going to have to face that wretched, painful heartbreak lie with a vengeance.

I flipped opened my notebook to a fresh, new page and wrote down the painful beliefs that were plaguing me:

- *I'm good but never enough.*
- *I'm never going to find someone else like Chris.*
- *This breakup is all my fault.*

These thoughts were incredibly painful to face, but at the same time, my wounded spirit was both empowered and fed up. I knew that if I were to let these thoughts continue to fester, they would eventually stink up all that I did, much like smelly trash I've often forgotten to take out.

The reality was that at the end of this break, Chris very much could break up with me. But did those lies have to infect my broken heart further? Did it really have to mean I wasn't enough? I felt compelled to prove my old patterns wrong and find a new way.

At the top of the page, I scrawled, "How to respond in truth if heartbreak hits." Then I wrote down what I knew to be true:

- *It is not that I am not good enough. I am perfectly crafted, a daughter of the Most High. God's love and plans for me supersede this rejection.*
- *If this is what I thought was God's best, imagine what other wondrous things he can do!*
- *Hope is not lost. God is setting me apart for something even greater.*

I could feel my soul coming to life as I stared at those words on the page, like a beautiful truth elixir soaking into the core of my heart.

I spoke the truths on that tear-stained page every day until the break ended. Every morning I'd open my notebook and face the lies I used to believe, lies that I was still vulnerable to. I'd let myself feel the feels for a moment (it's not about discounting the depth of our emotion; it's about pressing through it), and then I'd ask myself, *How are these words serving me? What story did they originate from? Do I want to stay stuck believing them?*

Then I'd turn the page to see the truths I'd written down to combat those lies. Over and over and over again, I'd read those truths with lots of love and a power stirring up within me.

I created one rule for myself: if any thought was self-deprecating, shame-filled, or fear-based, I needed to stop it. To recognize when something was breaking the rules, I had to fiercely practice self-awareness. That meant intentionally thinking about what I was thinking about. It also meant making sure I wasn't just going through the motions but aligning my inner dialogue with how I wanted to show up for myself.

Conquering your biggest heartbreak lies as you struggle to truly heal doesn't just require writing down the truths. It requires believing them so deeply that they replace the broken parts of your identity with new, empowering, grounded truths. They need to become *your* truth.

And to do that, you're going to have to transform your mind like a champ.

This is the part where Christians typically quote Romans 12:2, "Be transformed by the renewing of your mind" or 2 Corinthians 10:5, "Take captive every thought." They say these verses out loud like we should shout them with victory. It sounds wonderful (especially when they say it with a boatload of passion, sweating with enthusiasm), but my question is this: *How?* How do we truly take our thoughts captive and renew our minds?

I'll give you the answer: it's this amazing science-y term that I've come to love called *neuroplasticity*. Neuroplasticity is the brain's ability to reorganize itself and create new neural connections. As pathologist and cognitive neuroscientist Dr. Caroline Leaf says, "Our brains can change as we think (neuroplasticity) and grow new brain cells (neurogenesis). Using the incredible power in our minds, we can persist and grow in response to life's challenges. We can take our thoughts captive and change the way we think, speak and act!"[2]

Neuroplasticity is marvelous to me because it means that true change can actually happen in our brains. It's proof that God created our brains with the ability to rewire. It means we do not have to live as victims of the swirling negative words in our minds. Our thoughts are alive and dynamic, and the power to transform them is available to each of us. But here's the key: we have to choose to stick with it like a warrior prepped for battle.

> Conquering your biggest heartbreak lies requires believing them so deeply that they replace the broken parts of your identity with new, empowering, grounded truths. They need to become your truth.

Transforming our brains and growing new brain cells takes time. In fact, Dr. Caroline Leaf also says it takes twenty-one days to create a new long-term memory.[3] It is also said that it takes sixty-three days to create a new lasting habit in our brains.

This is actually one of the biggest mistakes I see people making when fighting the lies of heartbreak: they don't embrace the endurance to fight for themselves. They complete one step and fail to follow through to truly become stronger.

It would be like saying, "Well, I went to the gym for a week, but I didn't sprout magical six-pack abs, so I'm not going anymore." Or "None of the employers called me back, so I guess I'll give up applying for jobs and hope one miraculously appears so I can pay my rent." Or "I ate a head of broccoli once and didn't feel a difference, so back to Chick-fil-A I go."

This might sound laughable, but this is what we often do when it comes to our biggest mental battles. We can't take one step in a healthy direction without also grasping ahold of some true, honest-to-goodness endurance.

And if you think you can't have endurance during a deep pain such as heartbreak, I promise you that's a shaming lie your mind is feeding you to keep you stuck and away from true freedom.

Endurance isn't about coming in first place in the race, and it's not even about keeping the exact stride you had at the beginning of a race. It's actually much simpler than that. It's about putting one foot in front of the other over and over again.

So, how are we going to do that? We're going to constantly, day by day, choose to move away from destructive lies, toxic thoughts, and downward spirals and instead pivot to speak the truth (even when the old neuropathways are so deep that we don't fully believe the truths just yet).

> We have it in us— a sacred power that was meant for battles like this.

We have it in us—a sacred power that was meant for battles like this. We just have to take the first step.

Finding the Truths Covered in Tearstains

Finally, the moment arrived. Our break ended, and Chris had planned to come over to have the final conversation on whether we were going to stay together. He was supposed to arrive at 5:00 p.m. but was running late. For every minute past 5:00 that ticked by, I could feel my palms get sweatier and my heart race faster.

Kait, even if this makes no sense, Jesus has you, I told myself. *Remember the truths. Whatever you do, stay focused, pay attention, and remember the rule you made for yourself. Remember how you want to show up for yourself.*

At 5:20 I heard a ring at the door. I peered out my bedroom window to assess the scene. I could immediately sense his nervous demeanor and noticed he was holding something in his hand . . . what was that? A letter? Was it a *goodbye* letter? As the anxiety pulsed harder through my veins, I brushed away the thought and scurried to the front door. When I opened the door and saw the concerned look on his face, a strange and complex stew of emotions began swirling in my heart. I wanted to get the conversation over with, but at the same time I didn't want it to even begin if it meant this would be one of the last times I got to look into those beautiful brown eyes.

We sat down, and Chris asked me to share first. I had promised myself that I would walk into this conversation with strength and dignity, coupled with a whole lot of love and grace for myself.

As my inner mentor, Brené Brown, says, "Strong back, soft front, wild heart."[4]

After I bravely shared my own learnings of what I had processed, it was his turn. "What about you?" I nervously asked. As I gave him the stage, a look of panic filled his eyes and the color in his face quickly began to fade.

Chris started talking, and it became clear where the conversation was headed. This was it, time to brace for impact. I had my journal open to the truths I had scrawled out, and I looked down at the page as he spoke, letting the words I had written envelop my heart and mind with equal parts love and strength.

I am good enough . . . God can do wondrous things . . . hope is not lost . . . I am being set apart for something even greater.

As Chris delivered his breakup speech, the words I had written in that journal became my source of strength. They were like the very breath in my lungs, keeping my heart beating, reminding me I was still alive. They showed me I had a power within me to endure all things amid the myriad of lies I was feeling about my worth.

This is certainly not what I wanted, and I surely didn't understand it, but I also felt confident that I could be strong through it. And as painful as every word he delivered was to hear, I was.

Heartbreak is so incredibly difficult when it hits us in the face like a ton of bricks. It is jarring, painful, confusing, shocking, sad, frustrating . . . All. The. Feels. Whether heartbreak has just happened or we went through it in the past (maybe even more than once), we often think its mission is to wreak complete havoc on our lives. But what I came to discover in the throes of my biggest heartbreak was that it was there to teach me, protect me from the unseen, and redirect me to something I never thought possible.

I wonder if I could invite you into finding that same realization for yourself?

Maybe instead of seeing our heartbreak as serving only to highlight our insufficiency (thus spurring a floodgate of negative self-talk), we could redirect the script. What if instead we focus on fighting our biggest heartbreak lies with truth, which can powerfully renew our true identities? What if we hold tight to knowing that feeling the pain can uncover a new and profound overflow of strength and love within us? What if we cling to a hope for our future as heartbreak makes way for God to redirect our path?

If we allow it, heartbreak can actually be our greatest teacher, bringing about a beautiful new season in your life filled with hope, clarity, and comfort in the midst of unthinkable pain. I want to encourage you with some truths about the beauty of being redirected and finding strength through heartbreak that I firmly believe are true for us all.

The Six Truths of Heartbreak

1. Believe it or not, this heartbreak is protection.

Whether you want to admit it, you have blind spots that sometimes can't be addressed when your heart is entangled in love or care for someone else. It's possible the relationship seemed wonderful to you, but maybe you were missing things under the surface. Maybe it even had toxic elements, but because of the time and energy you invested, you wanted to overlook them to make it work. Just maybe, this heartbreak will reveal hard truths you need to face. Just maybe, it's actually *protecting* you.

2. Within deep sadness, you will also find great joy.

As hard as it may be and as much as you might want to put pain into a box, store it away, and never think about it again, I encourage you to embrace the season of heartbreak when it arises. The intricacy of life never feels as sweet as it does after living through the depths of darkness. I think of the Disney movie *Inside Out*, which is about our emotions, featuring two main characters: Sadness and Joy. Throughout the movie, Joy tries to make everything happy; meanwhile, Sadness keeps coming to throw a wrench in her joyous plans. The core message of the movie reveals something incredibly profound: to truly love and appreciate joy, you must also experience sadness. There would be no true joy without the depths of sadness. I'm pretty sure this is why James writes, "When it seems as though you are facing nothing but difficulties see it as an invaluable opportunity to experience the greatest joy that you can" (James 1:2 TPT). On the other side of your season of grieving lies a profound tenderness for and awareness of every special moment that floats your way.

3. This is only one part of your story, not the full picture.

The moments after heartbreak can be completely overwhelming and may even feel like physical pain. You might want to scream or cry or hide in your room, and at first, by all means, take that hall pass. But as you muster up the courage to take a step forward, you'll see that the intensity will fade, the pain will pass, and the hurt will give way to transformation. One day your wound can actually turn into a valiant scar. And (if you allow) it can even become a badge of victory you proudly wear that says, "I endured unthinkable pain and made it through stronger and more sure of myself than ever."

4. For every nope you receive, there is still hope.

Within every no, there's also a path to a new yes. This heartbreak doesn't mean hope is lost for your journey. If you want to be married, know that God has you exactly where he wants you. He has not forgotten about you. The extra time you now have after this rejection can be used to learn even more about yourself and the intricacies of your own heart. Use that as your strength, your motivator, and your fuel to be the freest, fullest, most fabulous version of yourself.

5. You can finally face your biggest lies of heartbreak with gumption.

Your biggest lies of heartbreak exist somewhere deep down. Like pesky weeds on a mission of destruction, they will infect everything they touch. Even among beautiful flowers, one toxic weed can multiply and taint an entire garden. To start getting rid of these lies, you have to acknowledge their existence and start taking ownership of the fact that they don't have to stay. This is the time to get to the roots of your biggest heartbreak lies, pluck them out, and finally align with the truths of your original design.

6. This is an opportunity for you to grow better, be better, love better.

Maybe not right away, but over time as you progress in the healing process, find moments to reflect on what happened. Ask God what helpful and wise steps you can take to be the woman he designed you to be. Too often we tend to place blame fully on ourselves or fully on the other person. Thinking in black-and-white silos will leave you resentful. Instead, graciously ask yourself what you can learn from this situation. Start to process how you showed up, thank yourself for the ways you showed up well, and get curious about the ways you didn't show up as your best self. How unfortunate it would be to suffer something so wounding and get stuck without healing, growing, and flourishing.

Remember the text messages I sent Chris the night before our "I don't have peace" conversation? The ones in which I told him he deserved better, in addition to other self-deprecating statements? How easy would it have been to blame myself and to have gone into an entire litany of self-guilt? Almost too easy. I would have likely shame spiraled and gone right back to letting the rejection of that breakup engulf me like a giant wave. It also more than likely would have kept me from fully connecting to the truths about myself, all the while blinding me from the beautiful hope that still existed despite the pain.

The destructive thoughts saying I was terrible or worthless or stupid or a hot mess and that it was all my fault were waiting and ready to attack. But during and after the breakup, I resisted them with all my might. I continually blew the mental whistle on myself when I wasn't following my rule, and I practiced replacing the negative blaming and shaming thoughts with truths about who God says I am. It was a brave exercise of endurance.

As I continued on my healing journey and met with my therapist (box of tissues included), I began revisiting the night I sent those messages and started addressing the fears and insecurities that still lived deep down within me. It was my opportunity not to blame or shame myself but rather to grow better, be better, and love better.

I finally began tapping into deeper buckets of loving myself, understanding my heart, and growing stronger than ever before. Though arduous at times, the fight for our own whole-ness is the most sacred gift we can give ourselves.

Glorious Ruins

Honestly, my breakup with Chris isn't the only one I've been through. I have been in the throes of a painful heartbreak more times than I care to revisit in these pages, and my lack of immunity means it will likely happen again. But the truths above still stand—now more than ever.

The song "Glorious Ruin" by Hillsong comes to mind as a perfect picture of brokenness taken from ashes to beauty. The lyrics talk about walking through a fire with your head lifted high as your spirit is revived in God's story. It talks about looking to the cross while our failures and ruins become lost in his grace.

They aren't just words; they offer potential, truth, healing, and hope.

It's possible to walk through the fire with your head lifted high. It's possible for your spirit to be revived, remembering that Christ has not forgotten about you and is *redirecting* you with his marvelous plans for your life. It's possible to claim that even through the massacre that's happened to your heart, new and exquisite things will grow.

> The more you spend your time focusing on the lies that come with heartbreak, the more you will end up trapped in defeat as a prisoner to their destruction.

The more you spend your time focusing on the lies that come with heartbreak, the more you will end up trapped in defeat, prisoner to their destruction. That's why you need to face seasons of heartbreak head-on. You need to feel the pain to heal the pain. Find the courage, embrace the pain with open arms expectant for change, hope, and healing to come. Day by day, ask for God to give you the grace to handle each day as it comes. You are in charge of how you walk out of heartache and into hope.

Recently, my stepmom, Karin, and I were talking about my breakup with Chris, and she said these beautiful words that sunk straight to my heart: "It's been so fun to watch you grow and mature in relationships. I hated seeing you in that place, but you came out so much stronger and sure of yourself."

One thing I know for certain is this: heartbreak is painful, but what happens after heartbreak is in our hands. We can't heal from it unless we feel it. We can't find hope unless we truly cope.

Sister, I believe in you, and I am right here beside you— tissue box, chocolate, hugs, and prayers galore. Amid it all, never forget this:

> You are altogether beautiful, my darling;
>   there is *no* flaw in you. (Song 4:7, emphasis added)

Dear Heartbreak,

It's strange to admit that I'm sad but grateful for you at the same time. I really am.

You always seem to come along suddenly, like an unwelcome acquaintance reappearing on the scene without an invitation.

Here's what I've learned about you: you're here to teach me, to protect me from the unseen, and to direct me to something I never thought possible. Every time you come back into the picture, I realize that by feeling your pain, I am tapping into deeper buckets of loving myself, understanding my heart, and growing stronger than I was before. It's never easy, but it gets easier. You've inexplicably taught me that fighting for my healing will always be worth it.

While you've hurt me, I can proudly step back and now thank you.

Thank you for making me face my biggest heartbreak lies, pluck them with vengeance, and finally settle into my true identity and design.

Thank you for the painful tears and sorrow that now help me experience radiant, soul-quenching joy even in the simplest moments.

Thank you that I can wear these past scars as badges of victory.

Thank you for helping me grow better, love better, be better.

I love who I am because, in so many ways, I've found my strength through you.

Yours Truly,
Kait

Remember These Things

> ⟩ Heartbreak has a way of affecting you physically. A broken heart can feel like a sudden (and unwarranted) explosion in not only your life but also your body. Both your *sympathetic nervous system*—aka your fight-or-flight response—and your *parasympathetic nervous system*—aka your rest-and-digest response—are activated, affecting you physically.

> ⟩ It takes twenty-one days to create a new long-term memory, and it is said to take sixty-three days to create a new lasting habit in your brain. It is possible to rewire your default beliefs

about yourself, replacing the lies of heartbreak with the truth about who you are.

> Heartbreak is painful, but what happens after the heartbreak is in your hands. You can't heal from it unless you feel it. You can't find hope unless you truly cope.

Ask These Things

> What is the current or past lingering heartbreak you need to heal from?

> What's the lie (or lies) you are quickest to believe in your state of heartbreak?

> What's been keeping you from facing the pain of this heartbreak, or what's kept you stuck in the grief of it?

> What gifts are in this heartbreak rejection?

Do These Things

> Tackle your biggest heartbreak lies. Take out a sheet of paper. Write down the top heartbreak lies you believe. Then next to those lies, reflect on the stories that formed those lies and write down the truth that you want to believe instead. Sink into these truths daily until they become seared into your heart (at least twenty-one days).

> Reference the truths of heartbreak at the onset of new heartbreak: stay focused, pay attention, and blow that whistle when you spot thoughts that break the rules.

> Write a thank-you letter to your heartbreaker (or to heartbreak itself).

CHAPTER 6

Now You See Me, Now You Don't

Fighting Abandonment

> In order to change, people need to become aware of their sensations and the way that their bodies interact with the world around them. Physical self-awareness is the first step in releasing the tyranny of the past.
>
> Bessel A. van der Kolk

I have something to confess: I *still* very much struggle with the fear of abandonment.

Yup, I said it. As you know by now, I am currently a single woman navigating the murky waters of dating. And let's be honest, #*thestruggleisreal*. Because of that, even though I've found the strength to grab on to my journal of truths and endure the heartbreaks that have come my way, I still have a hard time ridding myself of the underlying fear of abandonment that's made its home in the wiring of my nervous system.

While I was able to muster the strength to leave the breakup with Chris with my dignity intact, everything was far from flowers and sunshine and rainbows afterward.

After Chris closed the door on our relationship, the frustrating but familiar fear of abandonment popped back on the scene like an old bully I wished I'd never have to face again.

The thing about this bully who seeks to make us feel all alone and worthless? It's like he's not a stranger to us. Often our fears of abandonment run deep and began much earlier in life, usually in childhood.

The Abandonment Bully

I learned at Onsite that for a child to develop a secure or perfect model of love, they must feel balanced, healthy love from their primary caretakers. In this regard, the child must consistently be seen, accepted, and heard. But because so many of us are plagued by our own unhealed wounding—caretakers included—it's all too common that our parents didn't perfectly model love for us.

So, here's the scoop on the abandonment bully (yes, I am personifying abandonment into a bully, so stick with me)—he has many tactics. In his most obvious form, he can look like physical abandonment, such as one or both primary caretakers suddenly leaving. The painful and gaping sting of someone— such as a caretaker—physically disappearing can feel incredibly jarring and disorienting to a child. If this occurs in childhood, it can cause imprints on the innocent mind. The child won't even be aware that deep seeds of fear are planted in their wiring. This fear communicates a terrifying message to the individual that says "the person who was supposed to be safe left suddenly, so what might happen with people who are brand-new or total strangers?"

This form of abandonment is the abandonment bully's most obvious tactic. Someone important to you leaves, and you feel disoriented, grieved, and weighed down with a plethora of lies that over time engulf your nervous system with overwhelming fear.

Oh, but this bully doesn't stop there.

The abandonment bully has other weapons of destruction as well. His methods can also include someone who is physically present but *emotionally* absent. Emotional abandonment is just as devious and will equally solidify the ugly fears of abandonment in a person's (especially a child's) mind. Let me give you a few examples:

- A parent gave you a lot of attention but was not attuned to your specific needs.
- A parent was consistently critical, dismissive, or too busy when it came to your needs or feelings.
- A parent expected you to take on emotional burdens that were too large for you to carry at your age.
- A parent consistently mistreated you and didn't allow you to have a voice.[1]

Now, this is the deal: I'm not here to hate on whoever caused you this pain. I don't know them, and it isn't right for me to cast judgment on why they made the decisions they did. I want to encourage you not to hate on them either, or it will eat away at you like a toxic poison. We are all products of our environment. In fact, the abandoner may have just been doing the best they could while enduring their own hurts.

But the reality is, whether due to physical or emotional abandonment, these fears can develop quite early and then become the frequent programming we tap into throughout our lives. And if we aren't careful to face these fears, this abandonment bully can lead us to develop unhealthy patterns in the future.

I know this is beginning to sound bleak, but thankfully, amid my own dark pain of abandonment, I've found a glimmer of hope.

Remember in the last chapter how we talked about needing to actively fight for and have endurance to take our thoughts captive (2 Cor. 10:5) while working to consistently transform our minds (Rom. 12:2)?

The ugly fears of abandonment typically make their home in the deep neuro trenches of our brains like horrible monsters that feed on continual fears and anxiety.

Speaking of thoughts, here are some of the thoughts that typically play on repeat in my mind as soon as a new person— especially a love interest—enters my life:

Is this guy suddenly going to leave me?

Will he run at the first sight of my triggers and insecurities?

Will I truly be able to rely on him through the good and the bad?

Will he be able to fill the void of love I was missing from my childhood?

Will I ever find stable and secure love?

Can you relate to any of these thoughts, whether in regard to a love interest, or even a new friend?

What do we do when we have deep-rooted fears of abandonment? How do we live in wholeness and freedom when abandonment consistently knocks at the door? Is there a stable center for us to come back to? And if there is, how do we even find it when all seems so overwhelming and bleak?

Loved As You Are

Alright, it's time to come clean. I failed to mention a detail to you about my big heartbreak with Chris that I want to bring up right now.

During the breakup, I took the opportunity to group text six of my closest friends, who were all praying over the conversation I was going to have with Chris.

When Chris went to his car to get a blanket of mine, I took a big, deep breath as my emotions whirred like the winds of a tornado inside my chest. I could feel my emotional strength fading. I typed the words *I need to speak to one of you* and hit send in the group text.

As he returned, I could feel myself counting down the minutes until he would leave again. My face must have said it all, cuing him that nothing he could do would stop my heart from shattering into shards in every direction. Soon after, he kissed me on the cheek and made his painful exit out my front door.

Almost instantly upon closing the door, I let the emotions that had been bubbling up erupt like a volcano of overwhelming force and collapsed into a puddle of snot and tears.

On one hand, I felt proud. Just like Wonder Woman at the end of a long battle, I'd fought for myself during this painful breakup. I could look back and see how well I'd endured while finding hope in God and gripping a sense of self-love. And honestly, that part felt like a small victory.

On the other hand, I was devastated. It felt like a giant piece of my heart had just been taken out, and the gaping hole was undeniable. I have to think that maybe that's what it feels like to live out a Taylor Swift heartbreak song—that one day we would have told the story of us, of how we met and the sparks flew. But now, instead, the story looked a lot like a tragedy. The end.

Right then and there, the abandonment bully, in all his evil glory, swept in to kick me while I was down.

When heartbreak or trauma hits with sudden force, the fear of abandonment can feel overwhelming. Our thoughts often slingshot into an immediate downward spiral of crippling questions. Questions of confusion and frustration that can even lead to a stark doubting of God, wondering where he is in the throes of our mess.

God, how could you let this happen?

God, what is the point in all this?

God, have you abandoned me too?

In the moments after Chris left, as I lay on the floor sobbing into my arm, the feeling of aloneness overwhelmed me.

We were just together, and now he is gone. Will I ever have stable, consistent love? Will someone ever stick around? God, why did this happen?

My feelings of abandonment spiraled.

GOD, HOW COULD YOU LET THIS HAPPEN? How could you let someone else leave me like this again?

I began to think that unless a miracle of love swooped in, I would slowly drown in my pool of tears, swallowed up by aloneness.

But in that moment of utter grief and feeling alone, something shifted.

I recalled the text I'd sent to my friends during the breakup conversation. I reached for my phone, opened the group text, and scrolled through the responses. One of my friends asked, "Can everyone get on a call right now?" My heart leapt. I kept scrolling, only to see the response "I can" and another "I can," "I can," "I can." And then, right at the bottom of the message thread, appeared a very miracle of love packaged up in heaven and sent from God himself: a conference call dial-in number.

How could it even be possible for six women with insanely busy schedules from across the world to all be available at the same time? My wounded heart felt a glimmer of hope.

I dialed in, only to experience nothing short of the sweetest act of love and comfort from six of my best friends. This was my very own miracle of love.

For the next three hours, nothing exited my mouth except for sobs and a handful of hard-to-make-out words while my friends offered empathy. They listened for hours to what must have sounded like gibberish, they cried with me, and they spoke truth over my heart.

As I was sinking in the depths of my aloneness, I was being met by an outpouring of love I never thought was possible.

It was as though I could tangibly feel God's powerful, sweet, and tender love reaching through the phone and hugging me straight from heaven.

This miracle of love revealed something remarkable: God's love always prevails, even when we are in the devastating throes of abandonment.

Did you hear that? God's love always prevails through the pain of abandonment.

Here's what became sealed in my heart in that moment: God's love is *with* us. Sure, we can say we know this in our head. We may read it over and over in Scripture. But it's another thing to take that truth and allow it to coat our hearts.

I honestly believe that knowing this truth, solidified in both our heads and our hearts, is the first way we can work to fight against our deep-rooted fears of abandonment. These ugly fears tell us we are helpless, all alone, powerless, and unloved. But what if to fight off these fears, all you need is the most filling love ever known to man?

In Psalm 136, King David makes this claim pretty much every other line as he repeats, "God's love never fails" (CEV). Do you think David had moments of questioning God's goodness? Do you think he always, no matter what, thought that God loved him and had a plan for him through turmoil?

I don't know for sure, but I do know that whether David fully believed this to the core of his heart or he needed to remind himself repeatedly, something within his spirit knew he couldn't let go of the hope and power that exists in these four words: *God's love never fails.*

If we are going to work through our biggest abandonment fears, we have to grasp the deep and true hope that God's love never fails.

One or both of your parents may have left you.

A friend may have inexplicably exited your life.

You may have gone through an unimaginable heartbreak.

> If we are going to work through our biggest abandonment fears, we have to grasp on to the deep and true hope that God's love never fails.

You may feel like there is no person on this planet you can lean on for secure love.

But within all the turmoil, this fact still remains true: God's love never fails.

I don't want to pretend this is easy. I can hear your groans through these pages as you think, *But Kait, how do I really feel God's love?* Maybe right now you are struggling to feel that divine closeness. I totally get that.

But friend, let me tell you something: even without a grandiose miracle of love (like six best friends jumping on a conference call), God's love isn't absent. If you need some help sinking into this, I'd encourage you to start by asking yourself these questions:

- Do I believe God is a loving God?
- Why or why not? What evidence do I have of this?
- And then, finally, do I truly believe God loves *me*?

Don't just say yes because you think you need to say yes. That will turn into another science-y term known as *cognitive dissonance.* In essence, cognitive dissonance is when we lie to ourselves. It's when we say yes (maybe even believe we think we have to) when we actually want to say no, thus creating a lack of mental congruence. It also happens when we make a promise to ourselves yet continually don't keep that promise. We need to stop fooling ourselves and start being truly real even if the brutal honesty makes us face something we're ashamed to admit.

It's time to do the honest-to-goodness work of being fiercely and unapologetically honest with ourselves.

So, let me ask you again: Do you truly believe God loves you? Is there something in you that believes God is loving but maybe just not loving to *you?*

If you honestly don't know, what about starting simple and looking for little ways God has shown you love? Don't overcomplicate it, just ask God to reveal his love to you. If you can't feel it coursing through your bones, keep asking. The answer can't be turning away from a beautiful truth just because it doesn't feel tangible in the moment. You have a power within you to go into these places. Finding and truly feeling God's love means pressing into the very thing you need, even if it doesn't seem real and even if you don't feel deserving of it.

> Finding and truly feeling God's love means pressing into the very thing you need, even if it doesn't seem real.

In doing that, I promise what you're going to realize is this: you're actually okay with just you and God. His love is sustaining. It's filling. It's validating. It's life-giving. His love can carry you through.

People may abandon us, but God's love never will.

Victim Belief System

I know it's easy to slingshot back into our anxious abandonment fears at the onset of the next budding relationship with questions like, *Do I text them back? Do they like me? I'm enjoying this, but is it going to suddenly end?* But do we really want to be stuck in the icky mud of fear? It's not fun, is it? I know it's not, because it's been my crippling MO for so long.

Are you ready to get out of the fear and live fiercely capable of trusting and taking risks? I can't make you embrace what is about to come next. You are the only one with the power to welcome healing and freedom—a breakthrough in your mind and heart.

Are you truly ready? (And I don't mean ready like, "*Yasss*, Gina, I'm ready for my next blowout. Snap your fingers and make me beautiful." I mean ready like, "I'm fed up, I can't go on like this, and I'm willing to do whatever it takes to take my power back, do the work, and conquer these fears.") If you're really ready, I'm curious to ask you this: What might it look like for you to take ownership of the things you can control?

Here's what you *cannot* control:

- What happened to you.
- How people are going to show up for you in the future.
- What anyone thinks of you.

But here's what you *can* control:

- How *you* show up in mental freedom, clarity, and confidence.
- How *you* think, act, and live out your life.
- What *you* allow to rule you.

The truth is, you are only in control of yourself and no one else. Though every ounce of you may want to press against that reality, honey, your soul is relying on you to both accept it and then learn to walk like it's true. It's about time you step out of your own victim mentality, don't ya think?

No one is forcing you to be hostage to your fears of abandonment.

Stop and reread that. It's liberating!

If you are sick of replaying fears in your mind like they're part of a default alarm system, then it's about time you work to take ownership of getting rid of them for good.

Staying stuck in a victim mindset often forces us into what I call the *victim belief system,* or VBS. In the VBS, we believe things such as:

I'm always going to be abandoned.

No one is ever going to love me.

But I've been abandoned.

I'm too broken and messed up.

If only they didn't abandon me.

I understand why you got to the point where the VBS might feel justified. When the fears are deep or the abandonment traumas are intense, this belief system seems truer than anything else.

If I'm being honest, I've discovered that the VBS can feel pretty validating, which is why it's hard to change. Like the sugar high we experience after eating a giant bag of M&M's, the rush that follows can feel pretty good in the moment. But after the high dies down, we both know we're going to feel far worse than we did before. Living in the VBS is just like that. It doesn't actually help us get unstuck from the fearful thoughts that are suffocating us and wreaking havoc on your lives.

> No one is forcing us to be hostages to our fears of abandonment.

The next part is a real doozy I've had to learn the hard way. The kicker to the VBS is this: if we play the victim, we will more often than not end up the victim. It's a self-fulfilling prophecy.

When our beliefs convince us that we are helpless to heal from our past pain, we will fall into blame, hopelessness, a lack of confidence, and fear. And guess what? We will then most likely show up hopeless, unconfident, and full of fear.

I'm a big fan of flashlights, probably because as a young girl I hated the dark and insisted that I have one next to my bed at all times. I remember feeling empowered grabbing my flashlight in the middle of the night and turning it on to illuminate my room, easing my fears and bringing me comfort.

When it comes to living in the VBS, you know what happens? It's as though the victim picks up a flashlight and shines the light directly at themselves. How counterintuitive! Here is this perfectly wonderful and helpful tool, but instead of using it to help them see the way in front of them, the victim uses it to shine the light solely at themselves. This not only isn't very helpful, but it can also be blinding. And what happens when we feel blind in the dark? We get even more fearful.

You heard me. Self-fulfilling prophecy.

The question I've had to ask myself as I've worked to conquer the VBS has been this: Am I shining the flashlight right at myself?

This might sound a bit extreme, and maybe it is. But it's also the start of taking radical ownership of our thoughts and actions and getting out of the VBS.

Finding the Moment of Now

Let's say, in theory, you are doing a good job of eradicating your previous victim belief system. Now, how do you change responses you've been hardwiring for years?

First and foremost, you must enter into *the center of your fear*. I know you think I'm crazy. That's the last place you want to go right now, but trust me. As you feel your mind race, your body tense, and the anxiety ensue, take a moment to pause and simply breathe. This helps you gain a sense of security.

As you enter into the center of your fear, imagine yourself pushing the wound and, more specifically, your wounder out of your center. You do this so you can find a place inside of you that is open, present, and still aware of the current moment.[2]

That past memory and that hurtful person have no place interrupting the present moment, nor is there space for them in the hopeful future that awaits. So, push them out of your center.

I picture my hands swooping in and forcing them out with all the strength I can muster.

Now, hear me in this: you do not, in any way, shape, or form, have to *hate* someone who has wounded you. You might dislike them at first, but continued untamed anger will create a slew of incongruences within your body. If you are constantly angry, your body's cells will retain the anger and you will reside in a body overwhelmed by tension and angst.

In his book *The Body Keeps the Score*, Bessel A. van der Kolk says this: "Trauma victims cannot recover until they become familiar with and befriend the sensations in their bodies. . . . Angry people live in angry bodies."[3]

As you envision yourself pushing the wounder out, focus on what is going on in your body. Imagine in this center place there is a sacredness free of bad feelings. In this sacred place, you are safe. You have yourself and you have God.

As you push your wounder out of the center of your fear, next, I want you to find a calm moment in the *now*. Often our fears of abandonment send us into a tailspin of remembering the pain of the past or projecting worry onto the future. You (and only you) have the power to stop this.

I've heard it said that pain is an acronym for "Pay Attention Inward Now." I love that.

Instead of letting your mind go to past pain, stay present in your body, be aware of the moment, and go inward. Start first by paying attention to your body. What is going on? Is it hot?

Do you have tension in your muscles? Do you feel any sort of tingling sensations? Is there any sense of hollowness?

Bessel A. van der Kolk goes on to say, "In order to change, people need to become aware of their sensations and the way that their bodies interact with the world around them. Physical self-awareness is the first step in releasing the tyranny of the past."[4]

Seek to be aware of what your body is telling you (because even without words, it is speaking to you). In times of fear, I know my body speaks to me through getting hot, followed by a stark tension in my gut and often a tightness in my shoulders. How does your body respond in fear?

Once you can pinpoint what response your body is having, I encourage you to recognize what is going on around you. Tap into your five senses to discover and be aware of the moment you are in.

We live in such busyness, so worried about tomorrow or stuck in the pain of the past that we forget the sacredness of this exact moment right here, right now. Can you feel the wind on your skin? What about the sunlight on your face? Can you feel the breath in your lungs? Can you smell the fragrance of your home? What about the crisp weather outside? What can you see and make note of around you?

Stay with your senses. Focus on right now to calm you. In the present moment, breathe it in. There is peace, there is grace, there is hope, there is you, there is God.

This doesn't have to be a onetime thing.

That moment, the moment of right now, is available to you always, whenever you need it. In that moment, the future doesn't matter and the past doesn't have ownership over you. All that matters is the calming nature of the current moment whispering, "You are safe here, you are safe here, you are safe here."

This moment is yours to practice as much as you want, as frequently as you can. And it is your moment to treasure.

In that moment, you can find comfort. It is your secure place to turn to amid the fears of abandonment that try to overwhelm you. No matter what happened, is happening, or will happen, the calm moment of right now will never leave you.

> No matter what happened, is happening, or will happen, the calm moment of right now will never leave you.

As you practice using your senses to find peace in the moment of now, it's the perfect time to remind yourself of the sweet and bold truth we talked about earlier: God's love never fails. Not only are you safe in the present moment of the now, but you are also deeply, truly loved by God.

Jennie Allen says, "Taking every thought captive is not about what happened to us. It's about choosing to believe that God is with us, is for us, and loves us even when all hell comes against us."[5]

You may have been abandoned, and I hate that for you. I am so sorry. But the ultimate beauty is this: You don't have to be ruled by your fears of future abandonment. You have a choice to change them and work toward embracing a divine love that's always been there for you and look toward a hope that awaits.

Dear Abandonment,

Here's the deal. You've really sucked. Not just because you're incredibly painful, but because your aftermath seems to linger for years on end. This lingering has consistently brought on dark fears that have lodged in my brain, wreaking havoc. They have crippled the potential of past relationships. They have caused weariness about new friendships. They have made me doubt whether I'd ever be able to find secure, stable love in the world.

But here's the thing: facing you head-on, reckoning with the pain you've caused, and figuring out how to rewire this fear have helped me see that just maybe I really am okay with myself and with God.

I used to think I didn't have a lot of power, but the truth is, I do. I have the power to control me, to control my thoughts. Like the heroine of my own life, I can choose to find and return to a stable center in every single moment. Moments filled with peace, security, safety—divine moments that are mine.

I've come to even more deeply appreciate the moment of now. I've more clearly learned how to embrace the little moments: the sun on my skin, the breath in my lungs, the ways the birds chirp on a sunny day. I've begun to realize that people may come and go, but I don't have to spiral into fearing things out of my control.

Thank you for showing me this gift. Despite past moments when you've caused immense pain and planted ugly fears, I know I can always find my way back to that place where there is peace, there is grace, there is hope, there is me, there is God—and for that, I am grateful.

Yours truly,
Kait

Remember These Things

> The fear of abandonment is a real thing that's likely to happen after a sudden heartbreak, the loss of a loved one, or a failed relationship.

> Often your fears of abandonment run deep and probably began sinking their ugly roots into your mind early in life, usually in childhood.

> You don't have to be ruled by your fears of future abandonment. You have a choice to change them and work toward embracing a divine love that's always been there for you—and a hope that awaits.

Ask These Things

> What main fears of abandonment do you experience when new people enter your life?

> Do you really believe God is a loving God? Why or why not? Do you truly believe God loves *you*?

> What might it look like for you to take ownership of the things you can control?

Do These Things

> Write down your current or past victim belief system (VBS). Then write your new belief system as a way to take radical ownership.

- Practice entering into the center of your fear. Push your wounder out, find a calm moment in the now, and remind yourself that you are safe and loved.

- Write a thank-you letter to abandonment.

CHAPTER 7

The Dreaded F-Word

Fighting Failure

Our greatest fear should not be of failure but of succeeding at things in life that don't really matter.

Francis Chan

There came a time when I reached a breaking point in my career. It was late on a Sunday night. The room was dark, lit only by the blue glow of my computer screen. I was furiously typing, trying to catch up on the endless emails in my inbox waiting for a reply.

I remember my sweet roommate, Jessica, peeking her sleepy head out of her room to ask me, "Kait, what are you doing out there, girl?" It was well past the point in the evening when I turn into a pumpkin.

I peered over the top of my screen, opened my mouth to respond, and froze. I didn't know what to even say. I felt the overwhelm of overworking suffocate the words out of me. I wasn't even sure if I had showered all weekend. I missed my friends. My chest felt so tight, like I could keel over at any second of a heart attack. The wave of emotions elicited a flood of tears.

What *was* I doing? I was working so hard, but I still felt that I was letting down my coworkers, letting down my team, letting down my vendors, letting down my friends, and worst of all, letting down myself. I felt like a total and complete *failure.*

Through sobs, I tried to explain myself to Jessica. "I-I-I don't know."

Just eight months earlier, I had moved across the country to take a job as a senior buyer at a luxury fashion company in LA. I was eager to soak in the city's more chilled-out lifestyle. This was *seemingly* the best next step for my career. As such, I made a decision that seemed duly appropriate to commemorate this grand occasion. I bought my first pair of Rockstud Valentinos to celebrate. I slipped on the overpriced stilettos and felt like I had "made it."

But just one week into my new position, my I'm-so-excited-to-have-this-job high began to fade as the rose-colored glasses came off and I settled into some hard realities:

- Everyone got to the office at the crack of dawn.
- They stayed at the office well past sunset.
- No one really ate because of back-to-back meetings.
- They scheduled meetings *on the weekends.*

Holy smokes! Dorothy, we were not in Kansas anymore.

I had a couple of options. Option 1, make a mad dash for the exit with the words *Run, Kait, run* in the back of my mind or option 2, leave Forrest Gump out of this and do my best to put my head down, grin, and bear it.

I chose the latter. I kicked into high gear, pushing full speed ahead. For the next eight months, I worked my tail feathers off. I came to the office by 8:00 a.m., left every night around 7:00 or 8:00, and proceeded to work all weekends from home.

Sleep-deprived, stressed up the wazoo, and with my heart palpitating from my never-ending to-do list, I started developing chest pains and unbearable brain fog. I felt like an eighty-year-old woman on the verge of heart failure who forgot things I'd heard just five minutes before.

In the process, I naturally started missing things. I'd forget to reply to an important email. I'd make a financial mistake on a report. I'd actually miss deadlines for projects. Little failures piled up on top of little failures—all of which kept making me feel like I wasn't doing enough, trying hard enough, or performing well enough.

So, there I was on a Sunday night, barely keeping my head above water. I was drowning under the pressure. A constant state of chaos and exhaustion became my norm, until I could no longer ignore the tightening pains building in my chest. I saw a doctor and was prescribed anxiety medication for panic attacks and handed a pamphlet on breathing techniques.

Can we pause right here for a sec? Because I honestly don't think this is just me. No, actually, I *know* it's not just me. Why? Because this standard of *doing* has become our cultural norm, especially for millennials in America. We have become a culture of go-go-go-go, constantly working to go/do/be the next best thing.

According to Gallup research, here are some recent stats on millennials:

- Millennials currently account for upwards of 50 percent of the workforce.

- About 21 percent of millennials report changing jobs within the last year, while 60 percent are open to other opportunities.
- And 73 percent of millennials report working over forty hours a week, and nearly 25 percent work more than fifty hours a week.[1]

Do you get the picture?

Seriously, we live to work. Whether we're tirelessly practicing to be the star athlete, going to school to get our master's degree, doing night shifts and trying to build a side business, constantly networking to meet a connection that's going to land us the perfect dream job, or working seventy hours a week and fighting panic attacks just to stay on top of our workload, we've become more and more like human *doings*, not actual human *beings*.

I'm not saying working hard is a bad thing, but I do want us to get curious about *why* we feel like we have to do it all and be the best. Is it an aversion to failure? And what happens when we don't get the things we are working hard for? Is all of it for nothing if we don't succeed? Should we be labeled as failures if we don't meet our goals?

I'm sharing this with you because, friends, this is just as much you as it is me. But over time, feeling the weight of life's "closed doors" led me to question why we all strive for success and vehemently fear failure. As I went on this countercultural journey to dive into my inherent worth and value, I became hopeful that, despite all the worldly forces, there were some beautiful hopes and truths I could cling to.

Work Does Not Equal Worthy

If you haven't noticed by now, I like to work. In college, I couldn't wait to graduate and beeline it to the big city to start my career.

Sorority parties? Nah, I'll study instead.

Happy hour? Nope, I'll stay and work a few more hours and meet up with you later.

I'll never forget the day I took the Enneagram Institute's RHETI test. My test results came back saying that I was an Enneagram type 3. As I read the description, I felt like someone was reaching through my computer screen, grabbing my shirt, and yelling, "You've been found out!"

If you don't know what the Enneagram is, it's a personality typing system that has been sweeping Christian culture like the latest Maverick City Music song. If you've discovered it, you're likely at a point where you love it and use it to assess all your relationships, or you're #*overit* and roll your eyes every time you scroll past a new meme about it.

But for all intents and purposes, I'm a bona fide type 3, also known as "the Achiever." In essence, I like big goals, want to be perceived as well-liked and successful, volunteer to be the group leader, and will essentially do whatever to get the job done.

The biggest fear of a type 3 is failing. In many ways, their worthiness is tied to their ability to impress and appear successful. Like I said, I felt *completely* outed reading those test results.

I thought having the top grades would make me feel special.

I thought making it into that school would make me valuable.

I thought getting that job would deem me successful.

I thought killing it at work would make me great.

I thought being the top performer in everything I tried would make me *feel* worthy.

I was so busy trying to prove myself that I didn't have time to slow down and ask something important.

But . . . *What if none of this made me more worthy?*

I'm sorry, come again?!

When I began to ask whether I felt worthy, this question rattled me. It was difficult to admit that I thrived on the dopamine high that came through performing or perfectionism or people thinking highly of me. If I'm *real* honest with you, the shadow side of me likes being praised, likes feeling successful, likes feeling I am unique or the best at something.

But even with my laundry list of accolades and impressive endeavors, a much bigger and more important question was at play: Am I worthy or loved or more valuable because of what I've achieved?

Are *you* worthy or loved or valuable because of your achievements? We'd like to think we are worthy because of how hard we've worked, and our culture will certainly try to convince us of it. But work does not equal worthy.

Think about it. Have you ever seen someone's tombstone etched with all their accomplishments? "Here lies Amy. She ran a multimillion-dollar company, got straight A's on all her school exams, had amazing success and great style, and never failed in her entire life."

> As we seek approval for what we do, we forget that we were born with all the love and approval we'll ever need.

No. Because that isn't even close to what people care about when we are dead. The impact we had matters, and sometimes our impact can be through what we do, but really, it's more than that. Those who know and love us care about our character, our heart for others, the unique ways we see the world, our humor that can lift spirits in any room, how we go out of our way to see and show compassion. That's the real stuff of life. That's what sets you apart. That's what matters.

I believe that as we seek approval for what we do, we forget that we were born with all the love and approval we'll ever need. I believe that what we do is an amazing extension of the gifts God has given us, but it is not what defines us. I believe that while our work can be part of our calling, so much more is waiting around the corner of performance. I believe God's unique and perfect design for us is not rooted in how "successful" we are.

Our purpose isn't in how hard we work for this world but how hard we strive to become more like Jesus.

I'm not saying we shouldn't work hard, persevere, or create goals. (To this day, I get such joy out of a neatly written to-do list!) Those can be important things, but it is possible to work hard, persevere, and create goals while also not letting those things define us.

Author Thomas Merton says this: "Every one of us is shadowed by an illusory person: a false self. . . . We are not very good at recognizing illusions, least of all the ones we cherish about ourselves."[2]

When Merton refers to our false self, he means the things that act as a veil to hide our true, God-created identity. The veil of performance we discussed earlier that I put over my inner child and had to face while at Onsite? I lost the essence of who I really was by hiding behind the constant tyranny of performance.

And I know I'm only one swimmer in a sea of performers racing to beat out the billions of others in this world. Whether you're a type 3 or another Enneagram personality type, I'm guessing you've dipped your toes into the seas of performance too. Maybe you've hidden behind your accomplishments or looked for approval to affirm your value or tried to incessantly maintain a certain level of perfection. Maybe you've struggled to reveal parts of yourself, the parts that are true and beautiful and central to who you are.

> I lost the essence of who I really was by hiding behind the constant tyranny of performance.

If your job were taken away tomorrow, would you feel like your life has no meaning?

If you didn't get the role or make the team, would you beat yourself up and replay everything you could have done differently?

If your house wasn't as clean as those of the other moms from your child's school, would you compare and shame yourself?

If your boss demoted you next month, would you find yourself in a debilitating pit of depression?

Or how about relationally? Do you feel like a failure? Maybe you've thought . . .

If only I hadn't made that mistake, maybe it wouldn't have ended.

If only I was more interesting, maybe he would have chosen me.

If only I hadn't been so awkward, maybe that guy would have connected with me more.

If you answered *yes* or even *maybe* to any of the above, it may be time to press deeper into understanding your life's true calling, which is to become more and more like Jesus and less and less like a perfectionistic, workaholic, soulless human doing.

Let's take it one step further. If you're curious to learn how much your need to perform and achieve has affected your life and infected your soul, I have a fun exercise for you to try.

The Dash

I first did a version of this exercise while reading Jon Tyson's book *The Burden Is Light* (which, by the way, I highly recommend). Jon talks about how when someone dies, their life is represented on a tombstone by the dash between two numbers. He writes, "The whole of your life on earth is going to come down to that tiny little dash."[3]

That's what I'm curious to ask you, friend. What is going to make up your dash?

Jon recommends an exercise to analyze the turning-point moments in our lives. To start, grab a piece of paper, draw a horizontal line in the middle of the page (with room on top and bottom), and plot all the memorable, key turning-point moments of your life. This line represents your life from birth until now.

Before you start writing down your key moments, take a second. Stop. Breathe. Process and remember the moments that have impacted your life most significantly. They can be anything, and they should be a mix of both good things and harder, more painful moments.

Remember how we briefly talked about the Disney movie *Inside Out?* Clearly, since I'm bringing it up twice, I think it's an important movie. Think of these moments as your "core memories"—the things that have impacted the formation of you most significantly.

It could be that time you starred in the play or the moment you didn't make the cheerleading squad. It could be that incident when you were bullied or when you got into your dream school or had your first kiss. Think about the most memorable things that have impacted your life.

Got 'em?

Now that you have the memories, I want you to plot them on that line you have drawn from birth until the present. Of course, have fun with it if you want!

Here are some of my most memorable moments:

- Not making the travel soccer team
- Becoming first-chair flute in fifth grade
- Being disqualified from a beauty pageant
- Dating my first serious boyfriend
- Getting bullied in middle school
- Moving from Connecticut to Ohio
- Graduating in the top 5 percent of my high school class
- Studying in Paris
- Landing my dream job at Barneys New York
- Starting *Heart of Dating*

The point of this exercise is to look back at these defining moments in your life and ask yourself this: *What is the nature of the moments and things that have shaped me?* Maybe you're realizing that your greatest moments and hardest moments have been marked by achieving or failing. Is that the race you want to continue to run for the rest of your dash? I wonder, what does it take to truly live well?

Embracing the Noes in Life

Facing the noes in life forces us to come head-to-head with failure. And even as we separate what we do from who we are, we'll undoubtedly have to face the arrows of failure along the way.

Let's take it back to that Sunday of my breakdown when I found myself sitting in the dark, wearing pajamas, and working at 1:00 a.m. I sat there as tears dripped down my cheeks, hitting my laptop. I couldn't do it anymore. I was desperate to find a new way. I pushed my computer to the side, got onto my knees, and started praying something fierce:

> *God, I need your help. I can't keep going on like this. I'm tired of performing. Sick of needing to be the best to feel like I matter. So much so, I actually feel sick. I never sleep. I miss my friends. I'm miserable. I need a change in my life. Help me, Lord. Help me leave this job. I value this too much to leave on my own, so will you close the door for me? I need to be free. I need to start a new chapter. I'm terrified, but I trust you.*

Quick sidenote: don't pray for big things unless you are prepared for them to actually happen.

Five days later, I walked into my office on a Friday and got let go from my position as a senior buyer.

At first, it felt like a total slap in the face. As my CEO delivered the news, adrenaline pulsed through my veins and emotions stirred within me. My first instinct was to defend myself. *You mean all this work I've put in was for nothing?! You're just going to let me go?* Thankfully, as I opened my mouth to respond, I began ugly crying instead. Though embarrassing, it was a much better option in this scenario than overreacting in front of my CEO.

Once I had a chance to catch my breath, wipe my tears, and actually think about what was going on, I realized this entire debacle had God's name all over it. I had asked him for this to happen five days earlier, praying for him to close the door for me. He was straight-up delivering.

Look at God go!

Though the feelings of rejection and failure were overwhelming, this was unmistakably part of God's plans.

That night I sipped a homemade margarita, paced my kitchen, and cried tears of frustration and relief as I processed the entire week. I replayed all that had happened, trying to sort through my confusion. On one hand, I felt the weight of disappointment from not being "good enough" at my job. I felt like I had failed. On the other, I felt a strange sense of freedom and a calm in my spirit.

I felt God clearly impress on my heart, *Trust me. I've got you.*

Those were the exact words I needed in that moment.

I love what Katherine Alsdorf says in Tim Keller's book *Every Good Endeavor.* "My degree of success or failure is part of his good plan for me. God is my source of strength and perseverance."[4]

Not only was this rejection and these feelings of failure part of God's good plan for me, but my spirit was also leading me into a serene peace, knowing he was going to provide me with the strength and perseverance I needed for wherever the path led next.

Working so hard only to lose this stellar job taught me something invaluable. It helped me realize I had personalized and internalized the sting of failure as indicative of my inherent worth—defining how worthy or successful I was. But that was a lens I was choosing to look through. It was my choice. I didn't have to see it that way.

What if God sees our perceived failures in a way that has nothing to do with our worthiness or value? What if closed doors offer an opportunity to turn to him, seek his counsel, and surrender the plans we have our hands so tightly wrapped around?

God wants us to live abundant and free lives in which we're not constantly worried about when and where we might experience failure. God wants us to have enough tenacity and perseverance to get back up with our sense of worth intact when failures come flying our way. The question is, will we?

> God wants us to have enough tenacity and perseverance to get back up with our sense of worth intact when failures come flying our way. The question is, will we?

Want to know what happened next? Well, you're reading my book, so you don't really have a choice, but don't worry, I promise it's good.

The old me—the Kait who had been knocked down by rejection, believing she needed to try harder, put in even more work, and prove herself—would've updated her résumé, strapped on those stylish Valentinos, and strutted into an interview at another fashion company.

But this time, something was different.

I thought about what it would be like to step into another fashion job. Though I was good at being a buyer, I had just come face-to-face with the fact that my identity was tied to achieving at work. And let's not forget that the environment had worn me down to a crisp.

I was beginning to see that I could walk away from the bondage of performance. As alluring as another job in the industry was, I couldn't go back to that life. God had clearly heard my prayer and closed that door for a reason. While I could've easily gone back to my old ways, the curiosity in my heart pulled me in an unexpected direction.

Proverbs 16 says,

> Commit your work to the LORD,
>> and your plans will be established. (v. 3 ESV)

And later it goes on to say,

> The heart of man plans his way,
>> but the LORD establishes his steps." (v. 9 ESV)

Control has always been a problem for me. We can try to control all the things in our lives, but we can't plan away fear or risk or rejection. We will inevitably fail at some point in our lives.

What if trying to control every step so that we avoid failure only led to a life void of beauty and connection? What if failure didn't have to destroy our identity? What if it were a chance to learn how to be resilient in the face of inevitable closed doors? What if it opened a path to courage and vulnerability and led us to something better? What if failure actually taught us more than our successes ever could? What if it were actually part of the process of becoming more and more like Jesus?

What if this time we released our grip, embraced the fail, and expectantly waited with hope for the future, knowing we are no less worthy?

Failure Redirected

Facing how much my worth was tied to my work and losing my job were the catalysts for my leaving the fashion industry. It wasn't until years later that I began to see how God wanted to redeem this loss in a way I had never imagined.

Two years after this life-altering decision, God put a different dream on my heart. He started whispering within me that he wanted me to start a podcast . . . on dating.

Wait. I'm sorry, God, but you want me, single-girl Kait, whose dating life has been a hot mess and who is surely far from a dating expert, to start a podcast on Christian dating? Are you cray-cray?

Yes, I talk to God like this. He can handle it. I was truly in shock—either I was going insane or God was leading me into some seriously uncharted territories.

Now, maybe the idea of a single with plenty of failed relationships talking about dating was in fact a bit outlandish, but what I'd grown to learn was that often God's greatest blessings come from inviting us to sometimes lay down all our fears, step out, and do something kind of crazy—which takes a whole lot of crazy faith. The kind of faith that sometimes makes absolutely no sense at all. The sort of faith that causes us to step out, wearing a cloak of surrender, to do things that seem impossible. The type of faith that inspires us to step onto a moving train in boldness even when we have no idea where the train is headed.

I'll be honest with you and say I didn't know the first thing about picking up a microphone and interviewing someone, let alone how to actually get quality guests on my show. Who in the world would want to talk to *me*? My mind instantly scanned through a Rolodex of fears. *No one will want to listen to me. No one will agree to be interviewed. People are going to think I'm completely unqualified . . . right?*

The irony was that, rationally, the failure stakes were ridiculously high. God was calling me into something I had no idea how to tackle. I couldn't just show up with my fancy stilettos, dressed to impress, amazing résumé filled with credentials in hand. Quite the opposite, actually. I literally had zero credibility in this department.

But I remembered how God had brought me through losing my job just a couple of years before, and I couldn't help but think that if he was calling me to this, he would provide a way through.

When God calls you to something you're terrified to do, he will provide a way through it and teach you a whole heck of a lot on the way.

So, I put together a not-so-strategic amateur plan. I got some equipment, studied how other people did their interviews, blindly reached out to the top Christian people I knew who talked about this subject, created a website and a logo, and just like that—*boom!*—*Heart of Dating* was born.

Likely most important of all in this process was my willingness to release my idea of "success" for this new endeavor. Instead of putting such high stakes on the outcome, I chose to embrace the craziness of it all, living in the uncertainty of what might happen, while trusting God was up to some-

> When God calls you to something you're terrified to do, he will provide a way through it.

thing in the midst of it all. I asked myself, *Kait, if even one single person is impacted by this dating podcast, would that be enough?* While that went against just about every achiever bone in my body, I resolved to say to myself, *Yes, that would be enough.*

And guess what happened?

One person listened. Amazing, right? Okay, I'm kidding. It was more than one person. Actually, a lot of people listened, which was shocking enough. But the lunacy didn't stop there. Amazing Christian leaders, some of whom I had admired my entire faith journey, agreed to be on my podcast even though they had no clue who I was. Turns out I wasn't half bad as an interviewer. People connected to my stories and enjoyed hearing my voice, which was really weird to get used to at first.

Within months, *Heart of Dating* landed in the top fifty Christian-rated podcasts on Apple Podcasts, and I had people interview me to ask if they could be interviewed. With that I learned something profound: God's way isn't always the most rational way, but I promise it's always the best way.

It didn't matter so much if I was the best, or the most successful compared to others, because I knew that behind the scenes my God had the reins. His plans were working as I sat back for the ride. And in the process, my identity didn't become defined by the "success or failure" of this dream he put on my heart, the thing I felt called to.

Even if the entire journey ends up being an opportunity to bring you confidence, provide healing, make you humble, or give you unexplainable courage, it's still a gift to your soul that should be kept safe and treasured.

- You are not a failure, even if you experience failures.
- You are not what you do, even if you are good at it.
- You don't need to strive for a cultural version of more, even if everyone else does.

When you walk into something with enough strength and perseverance and are willing to face the risk of failure while also removing the need for validation and performance, something truly magical happens. You boldly take risks. You don't care if you succeed or not, because you know no matter what, you'll learn from the experience. You work hard—not to gain validation but to fulfill a greater purpose that's been put on your heart.

The ultimate truth is that, underneath it all, you are a gorgeous masterpiece, built with a unique purpose that's being carried out through every single turn of events.

So, the question is, are you ready to start walking through life believing that's true?

Dear Failure,

    I've been trying to avoid you my entire life. I've worked to do my best, be the best, and have control over every element of my future. I've set lofty goals and got my fair share of straight A's and stamps of approval. I've landed my dream job and climbed the ranks, all while never going a day without perfectly lined lips. I thrived on the applause and the early mornings with little sleep and being the one people always wanted. Perfectionism and performing were my crutch, my secret weapon. They filled the gas in my tank of achieving.

    Until one day, the failure hit so hard, it all felt too crushing to bear. All the things I had worked for came crashing down, along with my health and mental sanity. The fear of failure wore me down, revealing how I put my identity in fleeting things. Things that could never actually truly bring me purpose, make me happy, make me whole.

    I thought letting you win would destroy me. And it did a little, but in all the ways I needed. It destroyed my concept of purpose and replaced it with something that meant more, something lasting. It turns out that greatness doesn't come from what I do; it comes from who I am. And it also turns out that who I am is far more than being the best at what I do.

    Thank you, failure, for making me face the feeble, unreliable things I put my identity into in order to truly find my lasting source of worth and value. I still work hard, I still do good things, I still have goals, but I'm thankful that I've given myself permission to release myself from the pressures of doing and rest in the beauty of being.

Yours Truly,
Kait

Remember These Things

> You can try to control all the things in your life, but you can't plan away fear or risk or rejection. You will inevitably fail at some point.

> You are not a failure, *even if you experience failures.*

> Have you forgotten that you were born with all the love and approval you'll ever need? What you do is an amazing extension of the gifts God has given you, but it is not what defines you.

Ask These Things

> Identify a recent closed door you've experienced. How did it make you feel? How did you respond?

> How has achievement or failure driven your life? How do you define *success*?

> Have you considered that your calling is more than a job? How does that challenge the way you view yourself and your work?

Do These Things

> Plot the defining moments in your life (good and bad) on a horizontal scale. Reflect on how many of these markers were driven by achievement or failure.

> The next time you fail, journal how it makes you feel. Continue to document failures and your feelings about them, and reflect on how those feelings evolve over time.

> Write a thank-you letter to failure.

CHAPTER 8

I'm Not Crazy

Fighting Abuse

A woman could be smart, independent, capable, and successful and still fall into an abusive relationship.

Allison Fallon

It was 3:00 a.m., and I was lying on the floor of my shoebox apartment. My new burgundy dress from All Saints had been stretched out and torn apart. My bed had been pushed to the other side of my room. Things were tossed everywhere. My head was aching and pounding. Who knew you could actually still think after having your head slammed to the ground and your hair pulled out? My voice was hoarse and raw from screaming for help to no avail.

This was my status on a Thursday night in September—lying helpless, defeated, and battered, worried about whether I'd make it to see another New York City sunrise (or any sunrise, for that matter).

I never thought I'd be here again. Actually, scratch that. It had crossed my mind, but I hadn't wanted to face the reality that getting back with Scott, who'd already proven to be abusive, could mean I might possibly be in this situation again.

He could change, *right?*

Abuse is horrific. Whether it is emotional, physical, verbal, or sexual, abuse will deeply wound you and imprint a painful trauma in your memory.

I have to admit, I almost didn't write this chapter. And I want to make something very clear here: though the title of this book is *Thank You for Rejecting Me,* I am not thanking my abusers. There is not a single bone in my body that is even remotely suggesting that. But when it comes to healing from our past pain, I know this story is necessary.

Many of us are close to someone who has been abused or we ourselves have been abused in some capacity and maybe it's haunted us for years on end. It's possible that we have suppressed the pain or memories from abuse, keeping them hidden so they can't overwhelm us. Or maybe something has happened to us that we've excused time and time again because it is easier than facing the stark reality that someone we love is taking out their own toxicity and wounding on us.

Spiral of Destruction

According to the National Domestic Violence Hotline, more than one in three women and one in four men have experienced some form of physical violence by an intimate partner.[1] This can involve many behaviors, including slapping, shoving, and pushing. On top of that, "On average, a woman will leave an abusive relationship seven times before she leaves for good," according to the same hotline.[2] Man, do I feel the weight of these numbers. The knowledge of these statistics strikes right to my gut. It's haunting and heartbreaking.

My therapist once compared the cycle of abuse to being addicted to a hard drug. You know it's terribly bad for you. You're aware of its life-sucking capabilities. You might even know it has the ability to kill you. You hate it. When you muster the courage to step away, you vow to yourself you'll never go back again. And yet when the triggers and temptations come waving their hands in front of your face, it's brutally hard to turn away. This is especially true when your self-esteem tank is on empty and your ability to see yourself as God sees you is blocked by insecurity, fears, and doubts.

The statistics show not only that you are prone to staying or returning to the same abusive relationship but also that you are far more susceptible to getting into another abusive situation in the future.[3] It's as though the sickening pattern of violation somehow becomes normal to your memory as the victim. *Ay, caramba.* While you fear it happening again, you still somehow become vulnerable to those same patterns— patterns that, even though twisted, have become far too familiar.

When I was at Onsite, we learned about the beautiful rights of a child. We are born into the world perfect, beautiful, innocent, pure, joyful, and vulnerable. As children, we have the right to be, meaning we are wanted and have the absolute right to take up space in the world. We have the freedom to cry out and the right to have emotions that are seen and heard rather than discounted. We have the right to speak our truth and express our opinions about the world. And we have the right to autonomy with support, meaning we are allowed our own individual goals and we have the right to be respected for the choices we make.

We have other rights too, but these are some of the top rights that are most violated in abuse.

When an abusive person questions and discounts our needs, we feel invalidated. We start to believe that our needs don't matter—that they are insignificant, silly, and even a burden. If our partner criticizes or belittles us when we try to speak our truth about our life or even about how a certain scenario is hurting us, our right to voice our truth feels like it is being taken away from us. If an abusive partner attempts to control us by dictating who we can be friends with in real life and on social media, by isolating us, or by demanding to know where we are at every minute, our right to autonomy is violated.

> When an abusive person questions and discounts our needs, we feel invalidated.

Being invalidated, controlled, unfairly punished, put down, or physically hurt sends us into a spiral of destructive thoughts and feelings. We might feel ashamed, crazy, insecure, resentful, helpless, overwhelmed, used, weak, scared, desperate, paralyzed, paranoid, threatened, or endangered. Ultimately, this violation of rights causes us to question ourselves. We question if we are even wanted, chosen, or have a reason to live. It seeks to destroy our very first right to *be* that we were born with.

I know what it's like to lose myself entirely at the suffocating hands of abuse. I have drunk from the toxic waters of self-loathing, sometimes hating myself more than I've hated my abuser. I've been lost in the relentless seas of confusion, helplessness, shame, and, most prominently, fear. I know what it feels like to be trapped on all sides mentally, emotionally, and physically—where your brain feels too afraid to make a move. And I also know what it's like to blame yourself for it all, lost in a web of lies that at some point ends up convincing you that you deserve the abuse.

It's now been years since my abuse, and I've had ample time to process, cry, scream, hit my fair share of punching bags, ask

God the hard questions, and sit with my pain and brokenness in front of many trained professionals. Today my heart feels more compelled than ever to talk about my story and help others avoid what I suffered.

Picture me taking your hand. I want to walk forward together here, answering these questions right alongside of you: How do you start to recognize toxic patterns that have become normal to you? How do you break free from the chaos, pain, and wounding and come to see clearly and stand on your own two feet again? How do you put together the pieces of your broken soul after the pain and destruction of toxic and abusive relationships?

Love Yourself to Not Lose Yourself

Before I dated Scott, I had been dating for seven years straight. From fourteen to twenty-one, I had a constant flow of boyfriends. I was at the top of my class, an A+ student, the yearbook editor, a student activist, and an active part of my weekly Bible study. #blessmyheart.

Y'all already know performing has been my go-to mask. I performed as a shield to hide the pain I felt underneath all my shame scarves. Externally I may have looked all shiny, but internally there was a big ol' hot mess going on. My girl Celine Dion says, "Some people have everything; they have nothing."[4] Come on, Celine! Couldn't agree with you more there.

Behind all the performance, I felt like a fraud, terrified of being "found out." I told myself I wasn't pretty enough, I had an awkward smile (thanks, Aunt Deb), and my body was terribly unsexy. I didn't think I was smart enough because I had to work so hard to get good grades while other kids—like my brother, for example—could listen while sleeping through class and get straight A's (sidenote—if that's you, I admire and envy you all at the same time).

My internal dialogue had become so abusive that I formed some negative tendencies. I couldn't look people in the eyes. I berated myself with criticism when I didn't get tests back with a giant A circled on the front. It took me ages to get over breakups because I blamed and shamed and questioned myself entirely.

I condemned, judged, belittled, berated, and mocked myself. I enforced lies of unworthiness, shame, insignificance, inadequacy, insecurity, and ugliness.

I mentally abused *myself.*

At the end of the day, I was violating my core identity.

Here's the reality: if we already believe a significant number of lies about ourselves because we are constantly being self-abusive, the chances are high that we *will* end up in a relationship (of any kind) with a person who reflects those same messages to us.[5]

This doesn't mean we aren't powerful or beautiful or successful or leaders or that we don't love God. The assumption that all victims are weak and broken is an unhealthy stereotype that can cause further shame and keep victims hidden.

While I believe victims often struggle with self-love, it doesn't mean they aren't thriving in other ways. Abuse victims come in all shapes and sizes. While dating Scott, I was smart, successful, God-loving, strong, and independent. In some ways, this actually made it harder to share the abuse I was suffering because it seemed easier to stay trapped in denial than to share the reality that I felt would make me look weak.

Despite my façades and successes and other people thinking abuse would never happen to someone like me, it's true that relationship partners often reflect back to us what we already believe about ourselves. If we belittle and ridicule ourselves, believing we are unworthy and a burden, chances are we might be attracted to a partner who will see and treat us in those same destructive ways.

If we are not kind to ourselves, how can we expect other people to be?

I could accept the way Scott was treating me because in some ways (even if I would never have said this out loud), at my core I felt I deserved it. With every painful hit—physical and verbal—I found myself silently agreeing with him. Externally I was trying to defend myself, but internally I was thinking, *He's right. I am completely worthless.*

Maybe that's where an abusive relationship of yours started . . . in a deep pit of self-loathing. And if that self-loathing led you to look to that person to make you feel better about yourself, take away your self-hate, or fill the voids in your heart through how they loved you or saw you, you probably found yourself feeling incredibly disappointed—because humans will let you down—and, worst of all, more susceptible to abusers.

If you have been abused, or if you are realizing for the first time that you have been or are being abused, I am deeply sorry for the unfair pain you've had to endure. My heart aches for you, because while our stories may look different, I've been there too. Abuse is incredibly isolating, as though no one else can even begin to comprehend what you've been through. So, even if I'm the first to say it, sister, I am with you. And I am also hopeful.

> If you've found the courage and endurance to face these horrific circumstances and survive, imagine the power and resilience you will have as you heal and move forward.

If you've found the courage and endurance to face these horrific circumstances and survive, imagine the power and resilience you will have as you heal and move forward.

Don't Miss These Red Flags

There will still be seasons when you feel weak. There might be people who come off as extremely charming and sweep you off your feet. There will be moments when you are lonely and will do anything for companionship. And it must be said that just as victims come in all shapes and sizes, so do abusers. An abuser can be a friend, a parent, a CEO, the most charming person you know, even a church leader.

Because of that, I want to equip you with the ability to spot abusers with more clarity and discernment. My heart is to help you move forward in awareness so that together we can work to change the horrible statistics of abuse.

The cycle of abuse typically includes a period of building tension, leading up to a violent act, followed by an apology or remorse, and then typically a honeymoon period of love and affection.

The following are things I've learned to pay attention to as I stand on high alert for toxic people. I've found that abusers will often use the following tactics to first lure you in, and then keep you trapped in the warping cycle of abuse.

Red Flag #1: Love Bombing

I'm not going to say this happens all the time, but more often than not, an abuser starts off the relationship by acting incredibly charming. They are witty, quick on their feet, well-composed. They say sweet things that cut right to your heart and make you laugh. When it comes to a romantic relationship, the beginning can often seem like the perfect Jude Law and Cameron Diaz meet-cute in *The Holiday*.

This is exactly how you get hooked.

I'll be honest, Scott swooned over me, told me there was no girl like me, made grand proclamations about me, wanted to introduce me to all his friends. And because of this, the relationship progressed at lightning speed (kind of like those roller coasters that shoot you out at crazy velocity). Before I knew it, we were dating and I was in love (or so I thought).

Love bombing can temporarily calm your fears of abandonment, making you feel like all your worthiness voids are being filled. But believe me, a toxic love bomber knows it. They play the role by adoring you, treating you well, being charming and funny, and saying all the wonderful things you want to hear.

But while it might make you feel warm and fuzzy for the moment . . . it's a trap! (An alluring one, at that.)

Over time I've discovered something critical. When someone confesses their love or admiration for me, I want it to come after they've seen me at my worst or after I've had to ask for forgiveness for mistreating them or after they've chosen to listen even when my emotions make no logical sense to them. That's a relationship I can trust—one that's stood the test of time.

If you're the recipient of proclamations or promises before a person truly and deeply knows who you are, I kindly encourage you to picture a giant BEWARE sign above that person's head. It's easy to say pretty words but much harder to follow through with meaningful actions.

Now, it's true that not all love bombers are abusers wearing masks. In any case, love bombing (especially early on) can be enticing yet unstable. Often when exposed, early love bombs are actually false proclamations driven by the person's desire to control. Tread with immense caution.

Red Flag #2: Codependency

I first heard the term *codependency* a few years ago from my amazing friend Mike Foster. He explained codependency as a pattern of needing another person to need you, love you, or even change for you. Because of this dependency, you end up compromising. And what happens when you compromise over and over for someone or depend on someone else to make you feel loved or look to someone to change for you? Your identity meshes with theirs in unhealthy ways. Someone else's ability to love you or need you or change for you becomes a direct reflection of *your* value.

Obsessing over *someone else* ends up destroying *your* worth.

When I confronted Scott about issues that were bothering me, I noticed an initial pattern. He'd very clearly make it seem like the things I was addressing weren't really a big deal (violating my right to be heard).

Obsessing over *someone else* ends up destroying *your* worth.

Eventually he would promise that everything would be fine and that he could change. Of course, he would agree only after hours of fighting where I endlessly pleaded my case. Whether his intention to change was authentic, I clung with all my might to the glimmer of hope that he would be different. In the end, I only ended up feeling emptier and further confused.

Here's what I discovered about codependency: when we allow someone else's problems to dictate our happiness, we destroy our own ability to live joyfully and embrace the fullness of life. And you know what? An abuser thrives on codependency. In fact, they are actually codependent themselves, because manipulation and control fuel their pride. When they have you successfully trapped, their tactics are working. With just a few more hopeful false promises or love bombs, they will have you right back to feeling like you would never give up on them.

How do you stop the process before you're knee deep in codependency, feeling totally empty? How do you let go of false hope that a toxic person can change?

Here's the truth that has helped me finally stop getting involved with toxic people: You cannot, within your own power, change an unhealthy person. And you especially cannot convince an abusive person to change. When it comes to romantic relationships you must know this: you cannot marry potential.

I can already sense you thinking, *But doesn't everyone deserve a chance to change, Kait?* and *Why don't they care that they are doing things to hurt me?*

I get it. I hung on to many glimmers of hope with Scott, praying he would change. But the most frustrating and confusing thing about toxic or abusive people is that they don't usually have the ability to see that what they are doing is wrong. They do not always operate on the same level of empathy and compassion as other people. They have their own agenda. They are often more concerned about their level of power in the relationship than they are about hurting others.

The Proverbs outline three kinds of people: the wise, the foolish, and the wicked. Wise people consistently show you they are willing to be humble, to learn, and to grow. Foolish people are full of blame and excuses, and they often make the same mistakes over and over while rarely hearing you out. Wicked people are inherently evil, toxic, and destructive, and we need to flee from them at all cost.

When you are sorting through a situation with a toxic person, think about who you are dealing with. Are they wise and proving they can take steps to change? Are they acting a fool and blaming or making excuses? Or are they straight-up wicked and causing havoc for themselves and others?

To fight for ourselves, we must be aware of our codependent tendencies and consistently practice strict detachment. You can pray for a toxic person but you must refuse to engage any further. Talk to God more and confide in a close group of people if you can find the courage, but whatever you do, cut off communication with the toxic person. There are even incredible twelve-step support groups like Code that will help you sort through your codependent tendencies. But friend, you have to stop holding on to the hope that someone who has been this way their entire life can change for you.

It is not in your control to make someone care about how you feel. It's also not your responsibility to make someone change.

Red Flag # 3: Gaslighting

Have you ever found yourself feeling crazy, questioning yourself and being blamed by someone else? My friend, if you have, I have a hunch that you are dealing with gaslighting.

Gaslighting is often an abuser's favorite tactic. It's essentially manipulating someone by psychological means into questioning their own sanity. It's executed by discounting, trivializing, lying, denying, countering, deflecting, projecting, and even accusing the person of being crazy. Gaslighting is powerful and catches you off guard. And it often happens gradually, making it difficult to recognize that you're being brainwashed over time.

To break it down even more simply, I'd like you to reflect on if you've ever been told the following:

"I never said that. You're making things up again."

"Are you sure? You often have a bad memory."

"That didn't happen. It's all in your head."

"You're imagining things."

"You're being so dramatic. You're crazy."

"You're upset over that? You're too sensitive."

If anyone has said any of the above phrases to you, you've likely experienced gaslighting.

Gaslighting causes you to question what is true to the point of distrusting yourself. After the first case of physical abuse, Scott denied my accusations, telling me I was crazy and out to destroy his life. As time went on, I stopped fighting back. I started to believe him. *Was I all wrong about what happened?* I questioned myself incessantly. He was so painfully persistent that as the memories became more and more distant, I came to the conclusion that maybe he was right. In all my confusion, I fought for Scott like I was his chief campaigner, trying to convince everyone around me that he could be different. After all, I loved him.

Months later, when I found myself there on the floor of my NYC apartment after a night of horrific abuse, one thing was coursing through my mind: *Kait, you aren't crazy. You aren't making things up. This is really happening.* During Scott's tirade, I somehow found a way to crawl over to my phone and record the situation. I never intended to use the recording, but deep inside, I knew I needed it for myself. While being pushed and shoved and through a spewing of toxic words, my soul was screaming for validation. I was desperate for evidence that I wasn't in fact crazy.

Maybe as you read through these red flags you're realizing you have a close friend, family member, boyfriend, or even boss who embodies these qualities. Whoever it is, I want to encourage you that it is not too late to detach from them and find freedom. Continue to remind yourself that you will never be able to change someone, and they will never be able to love you or become the person you want them to be.

I also want to extend my deepest sympathy. I am so sorry for the hurt, confusion, and pain you've endured. I feel sick knowing you've been stuck questioning, blaming, and shaming yourself as I was. Not one drop of what happened to you is fair. You didn't deserve any of it.

Trust the Process

When my relationship with Scott was finally over, I did the "right things" for healing and breakthrough. I went through therapy and sought inner healing at my new church to really break the bonds of soul ties. I kept accountable to a close group of friends. But if I'm being honest, after a year went by, I didn't always feel I had to seek healing anymore. I rationalized that sufficient time had passed and I should be "good enough" by now. I felt like I had done the work and nothing more would really help. Honestly? I was sick of crying it out and processing it and feeling like a broken toy constantly needing repair. So, instead of going to therapy every week, I went once a month. Eventually that once-a-month appointment turned into once every few months, until I no longer felt it was necessary. I gradually stopped reaching out to pastors and mentors and started putting my performance shoes back on and pretending my life was normal again. I stopped leaning on friends when I had trigger moments and instead pushed my feelings down into a bucket that I could close the lid on and put it aside.

Enough healing is enough, I thought as I hurried on to the next thing.

The issue is, the trauma had been so deeply formed in my mind, that while I could function pretty well in day-to-day life and casual friendships, I wasn't quite prepared for the vulnerability brought on me by my close relationships—whether it was with men, my family, or even just friendships.

Years into my healing journey, I dated a guy named Andrew whose love seemed as genuine and deep as his chocolate-brown eyes that gazed at me with affection. We'd laugh and go on romantic dates. I shared my deepest secrets with him, and I felt safe. But one day, Andrew revealed his true colors. I discovered something he had done that didn't seem right and called him on it. In an act of vengeance, he verbally abused me and threatened to blackmail me by exposing my deepest secrets.

Then there was Alyssa. My best friend. The girl who would always pick up the phone no matter what was going on. The girl who showed up to my college graduation when no other friends would. The girl who sacrificed her international travels to take care of me when I got sick with the swine flu abroad. Two and a half years into our friendship, I found out the unthinkable:

she had lied about her entire identity—boyfriends and friends she had, places she had been, things that had happened . . . all of it was a lie. She had been manipulating and lying to me the entire time, using my loving friendship to her own satisfaction.

I thought I had arrived at healing from my abuse trauma and in effect closed the chapter of being susceptible to damaging and unhealthy patterns. Turns out the beautiful, ever-changing process of healing our hearts from the deep wounding of toxic abuse doesn't work on a fixed timeline.

If we rush our healing from abuse or abandon the process because we think we have come far enough or stop because we are trying to conform to a certain timeline, we might actually stunt the true, unexpected but beautiful process of growth.

In many ways, we will always be in process. You may not like hearing that, but the sooner you come into agreement with it, the sooner you can start living with a real sense of peace—a peace that doesn't just push out pain or hardship but is gentle and strong, unafraid of the unknown or the battles that await. The truth is, none of us will ever reach a level of perfect, well-rounded, arrived healing. We will get stronger, but there will always be more to learn, more for God to reveal to us.

At Onsite, every therapist repeated a saying to us while we were there. It's also a phrase posted just about everywhere on the grounds: "Trust the process." As cliché as it may sound and as much as everyone at Onsite laughed about how many times we said this phrase, it's true. Trusting the process is freeing.

I'm certain my words on these pages don't encapsulate your full experience of abuse. I'm sure, in ways, I've misspoken. I'm not a trained expert on this subject, but here's what I've learned to be true:

- You can find safety, help, and true healing.
- There is a way to trust your own discernment again.

- You are worthy and can find healthy, loving relationships.
- You did not deserve an ounce of the toxicity or abuse you endured.
- Hope is not lost, and you are not too broken.

You can become more aware and better equipped to spot toxic people. You don't have to be ashamed to have clear boundaries. You can learn to protect your heart even when things sound alluring and lovely. While the healing doesn't stop, you can embrace and love the process and accept where you are within it. And if you work tirelessly to love and reflect God's heart like a mirror toward yourself, over time you will be able to look at yourself without disdain.

Hope is not lost, and you are not too broken.

You are so loved, and your heart deserves to be treated with all the care in the world. I invite you to take the next step of fighting for freedom from abuse as you step into ever-growing strength and undeniable love.

You can do this. You can be free. You are stronger than you think.

If you or someone you know is in an abusive situation, please contact the National Domestic Violence Hotline at 1-800-799-7233.

Dear Self,

Let's start by clarifying something really important here, okay? There is absolutely no excuse or tolerance for abuse of any kind. You, my dear, did not cause the abuse that was so terribly inflicted upon you. You are not deserving of any abuse. I am so deeply sorry for the abuse you've experienced.

And I know healing from something as painful, as soul-crushing, as shame-inducing, and as identity-rocking as abuse wasn't easy. I know it was a long, tumultuous, and often painful road. I also know that at times it took longer than you wanted it to. There are plenty of times you wanted to throw in the towel. But, my goodness, I am so glad you never gave up on yourself. Thank you for making the daily choice to pick up the pieces of your battered heart and soul and seek healing. I'm proud of you for fighting for yourself even though the wounds hit deep and you often felt lost in a devastating whirlwind of shame and self-doubt.

In facing those wounds and pressing into the work of restoration, you were able to experience new depths of your beautiful being that you never had before. You dug up the areas of self-doubt and experienced renewed confidence. You faced the parts of yourself that believed you deserved the abuse, and you learned how to love yourself again. You allowed God to patch your broken heart, and you received endurance and strength in place of defeat.

Thank you for your courage, strength, perseverance, vulnerability, emotions, and beautiful heart, and for never, ever giving up. Despite the horrific things you experienced, in the end you discovered an even stronger, more beautiful you.

Yours Truly,
Kait

P.S. You were never crazy, you were never irreparable, and you are so, so worthy.

Remember These Things

> According to the National Domestic Violence Hotline, one in three women and one in four men have experienced some form of physical violence by an intimate partner. Abuse is multifaceted and can take many forms, including emotional, physical, verbal, or sexual.[6]

> The rights most violated in abuse include the following: the right to be, the right to have needs, the right to speak your truth, and the right to autonomy with support.

> Relationship partners often reflect back to you what you already believe about yourself. If you already believe a significant number of lies about yourself because you are constantly being self-abusive, the chances are high that you *will* end up in a relationship (of any kind) with a person who reflects those same messages to you.[7]

Ask These Things

> How can you trust and engage with the process of healing from abuse?

> What did you learn about red flags that lead to abuse that you didn't know before?

> Who can you reach out to for support in your healing process?

Do These Things

> Make a list of people who have potentially been abusive to you (in any capacity). Reflect on these people and write down what you've learned may have been abusive about their behavior.

> Identify at least three actions you can take to support continued healing in your life.

> Write a thank-you letter to yourself.

CHAPTER 9

Big Little Lies

Fighting Betrayal

Have enough courage to trust love one more time, and always [another] one more time.

Maya Angelou

"Hey, who's that Sandy girl who keeps calling you?" I nonchalantly asked Sean, my boyfriend at the time.

"Oh, she's just a girl from church. She's calling me about something we are working on for the Christmas service," he replied.

It starts with one small lie. A little lie built on another small lie, which is often followed by even more lies. Cleverly disguised as something innocent, the lie is kind of like a dollop of wasabi—you can't possibly know there's a deceiving bite hiding behind the appealing exterior.

But eventually, you experience the spicy sting of the truth.

It all boils down to one main thing: betrayal. That feeling of utter disappointment. The moment of thinking that this is not how it was supposed to be. Suddenly feeling exposed by something vulnerable you shared in confidence. Trusting someone to behave one way only to be stabbed in the back. The harsh awakening that someone has been unfaithful. A breach of loyalty.

Betrayal can be wickedly destructive.

If we break it down to its primary layers, *lying* is one of the most basic but common forms of betrayal. I think we all have lied about something at some point. Lied to hide something. Lied to make ourselves look better. Lied to avoid feeling uncomfortable. Lied to fit in with a crowd. Lied to please people. Lied out of selfishness. Goodness gracious, I've definitely done it—Lord, have mercy.

You've probably been lied to at some point in your life. Maybe someone told you they had your back but then abandoned you. Someone pretended to be an honest, trustworthy person and then left you in total shock when their true character proved to be closer to the wicked Prince Hans of the Southern Isles (I'm still not over how he backstabbed sweet Anna!).

Those situations are icky. Jarring. Deceptive. And at the end of the day, they make us feel *rejected*.

Breach of Trust

Betrayal fractures one of our fundamental human needs: trust. Strangely, it not only makes us question how much we can rely on others, but it also has a sneaky way of making us question ourselves. Before we know it, we find ourselves on the shores of trust, staring into murky waters. We may want to dive in, but we're not sure what we're going to get if we do.

That woman at church, "Sandy," who Sean told me about turned out to be a married woman with multiple kids who was having some marital issues. When the truth started to peek through, it became obvious Sean and Sandy weren't talking about anything having to do with the church service. Not even in the slightest. They were actually talking about spending time together. *Alone.*

Sandy wasn't her name, of course; that was just a cover. They both loved the movie *Grease,* and since they went to the same church, Sean couldn't put her actual name in his phone. Insert the brilliant tactic of using a famous protagonist couple as your code names—she was Sandy in his phone, he was Danny in her phone. *Clever.*

It doesn't stop there. Come to find out later, Sandy was being fooled into thinking I was an unbearable girlfriend, while simultaneously, I was being fooled into thinking they were platonic friends harmlessly talking about volunteer work for the church. Wow, deception can really fool us, can't it?

Finding out this information was devastating. When the truth reared its ugly head, I felt a slew of emotions. If I could put a word to it, most notably I felt *used.* And even deeper down, I felt unworthy and stupid. If you've ever been a victim of the rejection of betrayal, you know it feels like a giant punch to your gut. With your face to the ground, suddenly a wave of feelings rushes over you. Anger, emptiness, regret, confusion, hurt, shock, and even shame.

Here's what I've come to learn about the rejection of betrayal. It breaks one of our inherent human connections: *trust.* It can prevent you from believing in someone again in the future. It can also leave you crippled with so much fear about history repeating itself that you actually choose to avoid situations that even slightly seem like they could end in betrayal. And lastly, it can make you painfully question your own ability to make decisions.

To keep the rejection of betrayal from having the last say, we have to fight to face our fears of trusting again. We are better than our past deceptions. We can move forward. We can be wiser in the future. We *can* trust again.

I know you're probably saying to yourself, "Great, Kait, that sounds good and all. But how?"

Learning to trust again is certainly a message we've all heard. In theory it sounds ahh-mazing. But then you wake up and encounter more of life's ambiguity, and you're slung right back into a state of unsureness. It's easy to say you want to trust again, but *actually* trusting when your trust has been broken many times before is quite the feat.

Trusting again isn't comfortable. It's messy. It's difficult. It takes time and consistent effort. And even though I sometimes desperately want to stay inside my carefully composed walls of self-protection or bathe in my own self-pity, I know deep down neither of those things are going to bring me true connection or lasting intimacy.

> We are better than our past deceptions. We can move forward. We can be wiser in the future. We *can* trust again.

If we are going to live a life refusing to let rejection have the last say, then we must be willing to be brave again. Doing that is going to take a little discomfort and a whole lot of courage.

Had I not faced my trust fears, I would have suffocated the life out of myself and others. I would have shown up always assuming the worst of people. I would have continued down the path of self-criticism and questioning. And worse, I'd be rejecting other people, other opportunities, and other friendships in the future without even giving them a chance.

And trust me, I've fallen into those patterns far too often. I dated guys after Sean and went full-on Sherlock Holmes on them, analyzing their every move. One wrong look at another woman and I'd get out my spyglass, instantly worried they were going to cheat on me.

I'd fear friendships weren't authentic when a friend wouldn't text me something affirming after we bared our souls to each other. *Did I overshare? Was she actually judging me? Was she going to out my personal vulnerabilities to others?*

Living a trustless life is exhausting and limiting. There's got to be a better way than distrusting everyone, questioning every move until we are riddled with anxiety. *Right?*

Don't Try to Shove a Marshmallow into a Keyhole

I've found that the first way to move forward in rebuilding doesn't involve stuffing down your pain and pretending no one will betray you ever again. The pain from betrayal is often so big and so overwhelming that avoiding it would be like trying to shove a marshmallow into a keyhole: not very realistic or practical.

So rather than risk an embarrassing outburst of brokenness later on, begin by admitting there's a giant, sticky marshmallow of pain in your life (anyone else craving s'mores right now?). I've found that a great place to start is by simply voicing the pain you've experienced out loud. I think King David (who was not only a king but also the dude who wrote seventy-three of the psalms, so he was kind of a big deal) does a perfect job of illustrating what it looks like to cry out in vulnerable and raw admission of pain:

> But I call to God,
>   and the LORD will save me.
> Evening and morning and at noon
>   I utter my complaint and moan,
>   and he hears my voice.

He redeems my soul in safety
  from the battle that I wage,
    for many are arrayed against me. (Ps. 55:16–
      18 ESV)

Betrayal is painful—*beyond* painful sometimes. But like a deep, gaping wound, it won't heal by pretending it doesn't exist. And it also won't get any better by carelessly lashing out at the one who betrayed you.

In the situation with Sean, admitting my wound meant telling a friend who understood the weight of my betrayal. That friend was Nika. Nika had recently experienced infidelity in a relationship, and, sadly, this wasn't her first time. After deeply connecting for some time and countless nights sharing our stories over pizza, the parallels in what we had both endured were strikingly clear. I knew I could rely on her to be an empathetic, safe place to land. It's really important in this process to choose someone who will listen without judgment and love you with a heart filled with deep empathy.

By sharing this betrayal with Nika, I felt seen, safe, and understood. There is freedom in finally having the courage to be honest about our pain and recognize we aren't the only ones with sick marshmallow pain stuck in our lives. Sharing with Nika made me feel like we were a team and we would get through this together. Having her intently listen as I bared my soul felt like a warm hug that said I didn't have to do it all alone.

Confessing my pain also meant spending plenty of time on my hands and knees alone crying out to God. Sometimes the best thing we can do in the midst of a tornado is to sit still and grasp ahold of the most stable thing we can find. Though I've had many moments of veering from this, I've always found that nothing compares to God's consistent and kind listening skills. Makes sense since he's our loving Father, doesn't it?

Sometimes when we have no idea where to go, all we have to do is sit and be with our Father. Kind of like it says in Psalm 46:10:

Be still, and know that I am God.

Clinging to God's love and grace as I cried out in my own confusion helped me feel safe in the wake of my betrayal. Even though I didn't know the exact steps forward, I knew deep down he would save me. I knew he would redeem this. And I could be fully confident in these truths because I've read and understood his character to be like that time and time again in the Bible.

If God saved the likes of Joseph and Moses and Noah and David . . . why wouldn't I believe he's also willing to save me?

Whatever you do, pay attention to the pain you feel after betrayal. And when you're ready, share your experience with a trusted friend. One who will understand and shower you with empathy. Take care of yourself by going to therapy to safely process the frustrated and pained parts of your heart while having support. Pray and lament as you process your hurt with God, and let the reality of his endless love fill you up. Whatever you do, don't keep your hurt bottled up inside of you, waiting to explode. Ignoring a gaping wound will only lead to deeper infection.

Do You Trust Yourself?

After catching Sean in his lies, I realized another painful truth: I started to lose trust not only in him but also in myself. After a trust break, it's easy to question where things went wrong and analyze every detail, hoping we'll finally be able to make sense of it all. But often I've found that this only leads to spiraling into the endless abyss of questioning ourselves. So, here's what

I believe: establishing strong trust starts with a basic step. Being able to trust others starts with first being able to trust ourselves.

If we are going to work through betrayal rejection in our lives, we have to be stronger for ourselves. Outside of God, the main person we can (or should) always count on is ourselves.

Here are two scenarios that often play out:

1. Trust is breached, but we already came into the situation or relationship feeling unconfident in our thoughts and actions. This catapults us into further questioning and blaming ourselves. Without healing our ability to rely on ourselves, we risk putting ourselves in more precarious situations in the future.

2. Trust is breached, but we came into the situation or relationship confident in our ability to rely on ourselves and trusting our thoughts and actions. As such, we are far less likely to go down the path of self-questioning and can more quickly process future trust breaches with clarity, knowing they didn't have to do with us.

I've been stuck in scenario 1 over and over again like a merry-go-round that at some point makes you want to throw up. In fact, even in the moments I heal, work on myself, and move toward scenario 2, I can still slingshot back to a place of distrusting myself because of someone else's untrustworthiness.

Being able to trust others starts with first being able to trust ourselves.

Because of that, I had to really commit to repairing my own self-trust so I could be ready for life's inevitable twists and turns. What does building self-trust even look like? Maybe you are so lost in the weeds of uncertainty or have been so badly wounded by betrayal that your internal framework feels like it's been wrecked by a tornado.

Having a deep sense of self-trust ultimately means being able to rely on yourself through consistent actions. No more false promises or false starts that destroy your ability to be able to rely on yourself.

It means being kind to yourself with the words you say to others, being cognizant of what you're saying about yourself to others, and monitoring your own internal dialogue (it can be a minefield up in there sometimes, can it not?). It also means establishing strict boundaries and standing up for your morals and values, even at the expense of it being uncomfortable.

I'll be really straight with you here: it's especially hard to build self-trust on the heels of betrayal. Doing the work to build back trust with ourselves can feel really difficult when we're trying to balance healing and being in relationships with other human beings. It's not like we do the work in a silo. As the days and months unfold, we continue to interact with the people in our lives.

In a perfect world, we'd have enough strength to accept that what happened was incredibly difficult, but it didn't have to destroy us. We'd have the intuition to immediately talk to safe people to get help in resisting unhealthy patterns and finding healthy coping mechanisms. We'd turn to the right sources (such as God) for validation and affirmation instead of the looming alternatives. But here's what that perfectly curated equation is missing: after trust has been brutally broken, we are incredibly vulnerable. Our inhibitions are down, and without having already built a fortress of self-trust, our typical temptations and vices are waiting for just the right moment to pounce.

I'm going to shoot straight right now. You ready?

Here's what it takes to rebuild trust with yourself: keep your boundaries, stay true to your word, be kind to yourself, and be real with yourself about what you need. If you are always tempted to engage with someone who has broken your trust, then recognize your weakness and add strict accountability.

> Here's what it takes to rebuild trust with yourself: keep your boundaries, stay true to your word, be kind to yourself, and be real with yourself about what you need.

Have a safe person in your life who will check in as you work to be consistently reliable for yourself. Get in the habit of talking kindly about yourself and to yourself, and over time these habits will accumulate and build your self-confidence. If you have moral standards and personal boundaries, stand up for them. Practice stating your needs and taking care of yourself. Whatever you do, my friend, stay consistent in these practices of building self-trust. These will be your secret ingredients to surviving and recovering from any betrayals in life.

Choosing the Road of Trust

As I write this chapter, I'm sitting in my friend's cozy hillside studio apartment in glorious Vail, Colorado, looking out at the beautiful and vast snow-covered mountains. As I stare at the gorgeous snow-kissed trees and watch cars weave through the mountainous valleys, I think about how developing trust after betrayal is kind of like driving on an adventurous road trip. Trust is the destination—something we desperately want to arrive at—but along the way there will inevitably be a plethora of unknowns.

I believe that in learning how to begin the journey with our destination in mind, we have a choice to make. There are a few different ways we can choose to view the road we're on and the situations we experience along the way.

First, we can choose to travel with *blind trust*. You know those people who are so energetic and wild and adventurous that they will do just about anything without needing to know how it will turn out? Kind of like a type 7 on the Enneagram, who can be so down for adventure that they choose to wing a road trip, only to end up accidentally going two hours out of the way (love all you type 7s though!). Blind trust feels fun and exciting in the moment, but it doesn't always lead you to the best destination.

Here's a quick example to help you think about if you're one who hops on the blind trust train.

Last summer I started dating a guy who I thought was everything I'd ever wanted. We'll call him Chaz. Within the first month of our having met, Chaz was saying all the things my cheesy, romantic heart wanted to hear. He immediately came out of the gate with a slew of affirmations. He was intentional and verbally mapped out his desire to pursue me over the next year. He was charming and likable and a leader, and he even loved the arts (a typical *#swoon* in my book). His grand gestures and words made it easy for me to quickly get wrapped up in the thought of life with him (keep in mind what we already discussed about love bombing).

However, my mentor warned me that she saw some pretty big orange flags (the color of caution though not *quite* a red flag) about my relationship with Chaz. She wasn't on board with him actually being mature or ready for commitment. But in the midst of his grand proclamations, I was convinced that couldn't possibly be true. Sure, it hadn't been that long since his last relationship, but here he was laying his heart out on a silver platter, all the while reassuring me that he'd "do the work" should there be any bumps in the road.

But the reality was, the seemingly perfect situation wasn't safe just yet. Not enough time had passed for me to truly see Chaz's character. While everything about the relationship felt like my dream gift wrapped up and delivered to me complete with the perfect silver bow, I still had no idea what was really inside. I was blindly trusting this man without seeing how his character would stand through time.

Sure enough, after about six weeks, things shifted. Something happened in Chaz's life that made him unable to follow through on his grand proclamations and promises. He did a complete 180, and all his seemingly wonderful claims of pursuit and me being his "forever girl" instantly faded (along with my trust in him).

It's often human nature to assume the best in people. But assuming the best should never come at the expense of discernment or caution. There has to be a healthy balance. Truly trusting people takes time. The more we get to know someone and see how they show up in different situations, the more we can firmly put a stake of trust in the ground.

The second way we can choose to see the unknown road ahead is through *apprehensive trust*. We start down a new road with a cynical mindset, where everything seems sketchy. We try to trust, but we lean heavily toward skepticism and apprehension. We find ourselves gripping the wheel with uncertainty. We hold our breath around every corner, nervous about where the path may lead, expecting to be caught off guard or derailed. In the process, we miss out on the beautiful mountainous view surrounding us.

When we go through life with extreme suspicion, we ultimately miss out on the gorgeous connections that are possible with other amazing human beings. We live constantly fearful of uncertainty, which leads to anxiety and frequent second-guessing.

This happened when I dated Ralph a few years back. Ralph was the first guy I dated several months after a heartbreak I hadn't seen coming. I shared with him my initial apprehension, which I thought was justified. Granted, some of my caution was warranted, but here was the issue: in being so deeply afraid of future betrayal, I found myself in the middle of conversations and unable to focus on any of the words he was saying. Instead, all I could hear was a glaringly loud voice in the back of my head saying, *He sounds too good to be true, but he'll probably leave you like the last guy. He doesn't really like you—he's putting on a front. He has a cat. Don't trust a man with a cat, Kait!*

All I could hear was the doomsday message that no matter what Ralph was saying, he was wrong and not to be trusted. Sadly, my overwhelming inner voice kept me from truly connecting with Ralph. My strict and restricting apprehensive trust kept me from experiencing something potentially beautiful with him. Eventually, when one orange flag popped onto the scene, I panicked and ran the other direction.

If you're constantly finding yourself in a state of apprehensive trust, I want you to ask yourself this: Am I truly able to find deep, meaningful connections with other people?

Self-protection is important, but not when it forgoes our ability to enjoy the gorgeous snowy mountain peaks we are passing by. What could be a memorable journey of learning and understanding God's glorious creations can instead become a moment marked by anxiety and fear. We don't want to be so cautious that we suffocate the beauty, joy, and possibility out of every situation.

Last but not least, the third kind of trust we can choose is *wise trust*. This is when we accept that our ability to trust others isn't all lost, just maybe a bit bruised. Of course, it's complicated and takes a lot of intentionality and attention to build wise trust after betrayal. It's not one extreme or the other. It's holding space for the fractured trust we've experienced while also clinging to the truth that trust can be built and established with ourselves and with others. Working to build balanced discernment after we've been totally knocked down is not for the faint of heart. It takes time and intention. But no matter what, it's so worth the effort. You'll gain a sense of hope and expectancy about the exciting open road ahead, remembering the direction you want to be going while not losing sight of wisdom or caution.

I'm not going to pretend I have the whole "wise trust" thing all figured out. I'm still working on it, and if I'm being super honest, I think I'll just about always be. But I think there's a key ingredient that helps us establish wise trust.

The secret sauce in building wise trust lies in our ability to have *compassion*—compassion for ourselves, for those we know, and also for those who are new to us. Let me be clear, however. Having compassion for someone doesn't mean we offer trust unwisely. It doesn't mean we let a stranger into our home when we don't know anything about them. But it does mean we are willing to take them for coffee in a public setting and find out more about who they are.

You see, compassion for others allows us to still love people and experience them for who they truly are. Even as we extend compassion, we can still require that others gradually earn our trust as their true heart and character are revealed in time.

For me, the process of facing my fear of future betrayal after the Sandy fiasco meant having compassion and keeping an open mind about new men I dated. Just because a new guy looks at or talks to a woman doesn't mean he's going to cheat on me. And just because a man says all the things I want to hear at first doesn't mean I should let blind trust rule as I jump headfirst into a serious relationship.

Here's what I ultimately learned on my journey of healing and working to rebuild trust: not everyone is a deceptive manipulator, but not everyone should be instantly trusted either. It isn't fair to project past experiences onto someone who has never shown the same colors as wretched deceivers from my past. But I also can't be naive to the red flags of manipulation. Which means I have to be aware of my blindspots. It's a really tough balance but one that thankfully isn't beyond the scope of possibility for any of us.

Now, believe me, I didn't want to face my trusts issues. I wanted to stay stuck in my bubble of protectiveness, believing

I was justified in my intense wall of self-protection. But I was missing the beauty of life; I was gripping the wheel with uncertainty and cynicism. I've found that oftentimes the most beautiful relationships are the ones in which we fight for trust by taking the risk of a life of scary-close intimacy with people who have proven to be safe. Side note: Henry Cloud and John Townsend's book *Safe People* has helped me through determining what qualities indicate whether someone is safe or not.

There's an art to carefully watching someone's actions while also fighting to show up. Relationships should have a balance of both. It is possible to heal from past betrayals and show up cautiously open to, optimistic about, and full of compassion for people we meet and situations we encounter. Does it mean we'll never be hurt? No. Relationships are messy and people are imperfect. But here's the thing: we can experience freedom from betrayal rejection

> Fully loving and truly living can be the riskiest yet most rewarding gift there is.

if we allow ourselves to face what happened, fight for self-trust, and chose to move forward on the path of wise trust.

And don't forget to throw yourself some grace in this process. I have better tools than I used to in the area of trust, but I still veer off course sometimes. All we can hope for is to do our best and to have compassion for ourselves when things don't go exactly as we hoped. It's not easy, because relationships take risk. But I've found that fully loving and truly living can be the riskiest yet most rewarding gift there is.

Now, how about that adventure?

Dear Betrayal,

I have to hand it to you—you've done a pretty good job of stinging me in the past. You've made me question how much I truly trust myself, and, in turn, it's led me to doubt my trust for others. You're a tricky one to navigate, and you often come completely out of left field.

But, at the same time, I want to thank you for a few things. First, thank you for helping me learn how to choose the path of wise trust. I don't want to constantly run down the road of blind trust, assuming the best in people who haven't consistently shown up for me. I also don't want to be so suffocated by continual apprehensive trust that I miss the joyous opportunities passing by me. I'm thankful to be aware of these tendencies and feel empowered that there is a third route: the road of wise trust.

Thank you for also helping me reestablish strong, consistent, reliable trust with myself. I'm committed more than ever to doing what I say I am going to do. I'm committed to believing in myself and my decisions. I'm also committed to setting boundaries when I need them and asking for what I need.

Betrayal, you weren't that fun to deal with, but I can finally see the gold that you provided in my life. Learning how to trust in healthy ways is a skill I've always needed. Thank you for helping me unlock the secrets of that tool and for helping me fight for it like never before.

Yours truly,
Kait

Remember These Things

> Deception and lying cause you to experience the rejection of betrayal, which breaks trust and fractures the foundation of your relationship with yourself and others.

> Betrayal is beyond painful, but you won't heal from it by pretending it doesn't exist or by carelessly lashing out at the person who betrayed you. Instead, you can experience freedom from betrayal rejection by facing what happened, fighting for self-trust, and choosing the path of wise trust.

> Having a deep sense of self-trust ultimately means being able to rely on your own word through consistent, reliable actions.

Ask These Things

> What has made you felt betrayed before? Why did it sting so badly?

> What steps can you take to build back trust for yourself?

> Which road of trust have you often chosen in the past for others? Why?

> How can you choose wise trust in the future?

Do These Things

> Acknowledge your pain of past betrayal(s): journal it, say it out loud, tell a friend who can have compassion and empathy for your betrayal, and talk to God.

> Share your trust tendencies with a safe source, and set up systems of accountability.

> Write a thank-you letter to betrayal.

CHAPTER 10

All by Myself

Fighting FOMO

How dangerous it is when our souls are gasping for God
but we're too distracted flirting with the world to notice.

Lysa TerKeurst

"Yes, of course I'll come. Wouldn't miss it for the world."

Anyone know this phrase all too well? I sure do.

These words frequently fell from my lips after being invited
to something. Knowing my name was on the guest list for parties, weekend adventures, or even low-key get-togethers made
me feel alive—I felt *wanted* and *desired*.

Oh, heck no, I wasn't going to turn down an invite! Being
included held far too much weight. So, I said yes to everything,
even if it meant I was overextended and overcommitted. This

habit of being the yes girl got especially unmanageable in my NYC days.

After moving to the Big Apple, it didn't take long for me to adapt to the city's fast-paced rhythms. There was something to do every night of the week, and you best believe I lived it up, trying to embrace the hustle-filled identity of a true New Yorker. After finding myself in a community of women at a church in the city, even more events flooded in. Between Bible studies and happy hours and weekend trips for apple picking or beaching, my schedule was chock-full.

I'd work my ten-hour day in fashion and head off to the adventure of the evening. Living the true New Yorker way meant a girl in her twenties could survive on five hours of sleep and still thrive in her work, social, and romantic lives, right? I mean, who needs sleep anyway? (So said my naive twenty-three-year-old, I-can-do-anything self.)

Let me be clear about something: I didn't just go to these events, I *showed up* for these events. I'd down an espresso for an extra boost of energy and slap on a radiant smile, ready to meet people with charisma. I walked into parties or birthday gatherings or even church events as if it were "game time," with Beyoncé's "Run the World" narrating my every step.

You can do this, Kait. They're all going to love you. I'd pump myself up before I walked in the door.

Here's my logic from that season: Get invited to events. Gather all the charming charisma I could muster and do my best to impress people at said events. Get more opportunities to attend even more elaborate, exciting events. Attend those events and "kill it" once again. End game: feel energized, connected, and desired.

There was one minor problem. I could not physically go to every single thing I was invited to. Sure, Beyoncé has the same number of hours in the day as I do, but, girl, I do not have a driver or a bougie hair and makeup team waiting on me hand

and foot. And on top of that, Elon Musk hadn't developed teleportation yet, so this social butterfly was at max capacity.

But let's be really honest, shall we? This wasn't about whether I could attend an event; it was about knowing I was invited—I was craving (er, I mean, needing) the ego boost of knowing I was wanted.

I had spent so much of my life feeling sucker punched every time I found out someone got an invite to something that I didn't. In those moments, my anxiety would cue up, and I would find myself caught in an obsessive cycle of checking my texts and refreshing my email, hoping to see an invite. Where could I be found on the day of the event I had been excluded from? Likely sitting teary-eyed with mascara running down my face and aimlessly scrolling through all the Instagram stories of people laughing and posing, living their best life.

The rejection I felt from being left out didn't just conjure up a feeling; it created an entire hostile dialogue within my brain. *I'm missing out. I'm not wanted. I'm all alone.*

By putting my value in being invited, I was acutely aware of the times I was *uninvited.* Feeling left out of something I knew everyone else was a part of made me feel inferior, forgotten, and ultimately rejected. It defined me.

After three years of going through this exhausting social cycle in NYC, I found myself in an interesting position. While I expected to feel energized, connected, and desired, I was actually emotionally spent, physically exhausted, and still hustling to be wanted and included.

The culture said I needed to be invited and a part of all the things in order to be worthy, but after all that work, I didn't feel that way. I wasn't rested or connected to myself or enjoying a sense of belonging. The math wasn't quite adding up. I'm not going to claim to have a genius IQ, but as a person with a need to flourish, it was evident that the formula I was living out just wasn't serving me.

The Joy of Missing Out

Today's culture lures us into the fear of missing out (FOMO) so that we act impulsively. FOMO causes us to buy more, attend more, travel more, learn more, and be more, causing more anxiety and more exhaustion. It's an endless cycle of looking for the next fix to feel included, successful, and wanted.

Do you even know what you are missing out on right now by reading this book? While you are sitting here reading these pages, the girl you admire with her amazing thigh gap and perfect skin is on Facebook posting about the avocado toast she just ate with four girls you know at some trendy brunch spot in town (and after our latest global pandemic, who wants to miss an opportunity for *#sundayfunday* brunch, am I right?). Also during this time, someone in Japan probably invented something techy and cool (as the Japanese do). Or a political figure tweeted about something absurd and everyone is up in arms about it, resulting in a nail-biting Twitter war. Or maybe the Spice Girls just announced their reunion and surprise release of a brand-new album called *The Future Is Spice*, and you're going to be the last to know. (But honestly, I'm really banking on that one. Come through, Spice Girls!)

And here you are, reading and possibly experiencing a surge of FOMO.

Stripping away the need for that kind of validation took a major reckoning for me. Being invited and in the know had been my lifeline. I had a hunch it was time to be okay facing the rejection of being left out, but it was more than a little terrifying.

Maybe you've found yourself in a similar cycle. You recognize a need to be included because you just can't face being left out and the weight of feelings that ensue. Maybe you justify the need to be a part of "xyz" for one reason or another.

These cycles steal our worthiness and perpetuate exhausting patterns. What if being left out is actually God's way of gifting us the secret treasure of quality time with ourselves? What if it's an invitation to rest? Could it be time to face our feelings of rejection from being left out?

It probably won't come as a surprise to you that the biggest culprits of FOMO happen to be our smartphones. Admittedly, "My name is Kait, and I am a phone addict." That's right, I'm a bona fide modern millennial woman addicted to my device. Last I checked, it was an average of seven hours a day and counting (hey, don't judge!). I'm doing my best to implement boundaries and remove temptations while constantly fighting the intoxicating pull of instant gratification and the need to consume more. If you're a millennial or Gen Z-er, the odds are incredibly high that you can empathize with this problem.

> What if being left out is actually God's way of gifting us the secret treasure of quality time with ourselves?

Before the digital revolution in 2000, our attention span as humans was twelve seconds. It has since dropped to eight seconds. And guess what's even more jarring? A goldfish has an attention span of nine seconds.[1]

Um . . . is anyone else concerned? Houston, we have a problem if a tiny golden fish is beating us (insert face-palm).

The thing constantly keeping us up to date with new messages, emails, weather changes, Instagram updates, or breaking news is also the thing that is poisoning us with soul-sucking FOMO. Listen, I never thought posting a photo of mushy green avocado toast for the world to see on Instagram would be a good idea until everyone started doing it, complete with the hashtags *#brunchtime #avotoast #sundayfunday*. I also never wanted to see what I looked like as an old, wrinkled woman until FaceApp suddenly had everyone turning their youthful selves into old geezers and posting the pictures publicly. Now

I am scarred for life knowing what I'll will look like at eighty. Thanks a lot, FOMO.

Some people will argue that FOMO can be good because it motivates us out of our comfort zones to do new and creative things, meet new people, or work on projects we never thought we had the credibility to start. But while motivation is healthy, I also caution against motivation that's driven by fear. And that is exactly what FOMO is—the *fear* of missing out. It's fear that drives us to act when FOMO is part of the picture.

Because FOMO was so ingrained in my thinking, when I felt behind or out of the loop or uninvited, I got terrible anxiety. I found myself in downward mental spirals, wondering why I wasn't good enough to be included or contemplating why I was out of the loop.

Constantly feeding the FOMO while living in NYC led me to overcommit, under-rest, run from my anxiety, and lose any sense of contentment in the present moment. Over time, it led me to be disconnected from myself and deeply unhappy. By the end of my time in NYC, I faced chronic illness and autoimmune disease, mainly driven by my lifestyle that was chock-full of stress, constant activity, and a lack of rest. FOMO was physically making me sick.

I'll never forget the words my doctor shared with me after taking a myriad of tests. He said, "Kait, I can give you all the supplements in the world, but none of it will make a dent in your imbalances unless you commit to changing your lifestyle."

Well, that was it. The so-called disease of FOMO had gotten the best of me and had to go, as my health depended on it. I had become so obsessed with the FOMO culture that I'd run myself dry.

Based on my personal life experience and a bunch of research from some very smart people, I am convinced that trying to be part of everything that's going on doesn't actually improve our overall quality of life. It slowly eats away at our health, our sense of worth and significance, and our ability to be present and satisfied in the moment.

So, what if we fought FOMO with something else? What if we fought it with something you may have heard of: the *joy* of missing out? JOMO.

I first heard the term from Brené Brown, but it's also been used by the phenomenal Tonya Dalton, who wrote a book on the subject,[2] and the lovely Christina Crook, who created an entire community around it.

What if we got rid of our FOMO addiction and instead created a new JOMO mission? And what if our JOMO mission looked something like this:

JOMO MISSION STATEMENT

I will gladly miss out on things for the sake of staying more deeply connected to myself.

I will say no more often and prioritize rest and rejuvenation as core elements of my overall wellness.

I will fight the urge to fear what I am missing out on by staying present in the moment and grateful for where I am, who I am, and who I am surrounded by.

I will joyfully boast that I am not always in the know and haven't been to all the latest events, and that's okay.

I will view not being invited as an opportunity for something different, even if just to savor the now.

As counterintuitive as it might seem, fighting the urge to fall into the trap of FOMO and embracing the status of "not knowing" allows us to live fuller, more content and present lives.

As I started to transition my way from FOMO and into JOMO, part of this journey meant I had to release things I actually really loved doing. My new mantra when it came to living a life of JOMO and in the process growing closer to myself looked like having a very specific internal dialogue.

Repeat after me: *If it's not a heck yes, it's a no.* You read that right! If someone asks you to be a part of something, unless your instant gut reaction is *Heck yes, I genuinely want to be a part of that,* then you can say no to whatever that thing is. This is not always an easy practice, but if you want to have a higher attention span than a goldfish, and if you truly want more rest for your soul, it's worth a shot.

At first saying no when it isn't a "heck yes!" can sound hesitant and timid: "S-s-s-sorry I w-w-w-on't be able to come." For me, it was so difficult to just get the words out of my mouth! But, believe me, there is profound power in saying no as a weapon against FOMO. Instead of needing to go to all the things, and instead of having to know all the things, let fighting FOMO with your noes be your superpower.

Here's what I've found:

You are no less worthy if you say no.

You are no more valuable if you get invited or go to that event.

You are no more important if you always stay up to date with the latest pop culture and news trends.

You are worthy and valuable and important simply because God created you that way. You are his beloved. Your life has innate purpose and meaning. You have unique intricacies that make you truly the only one of you. You matter. None of this is up for debate, especially not when it comes to whether you are invited to or you attend an event.

> Going to less means you can be present to more. More present with the current moment, more present with others, and even more present with yourself.

Guess what? Going to less means you can be present to more. More present with the current moment, more present with others, and even more present with yourself.

The Myth of Alone Time

Far worse than anxiously trying to always be included or living in fear of not being invited was the agony of facing alone time . . . oh, the horror! Welcome to the bane of my existence—having absolutely no clue what to do in those moments by myself. The nights when I had no plans, I ended up nervously pacing my room or avoiding going home because time alone seemed extra daunting, almost scary. At first, being alone didn't make me feel powerful or connected to myself. It just made me feel left out, miserable, and rejected.

As I started on the journey to say no to more and embrace JOMO in my life, I knew I couldn't avoid it any longer . . . it was time to face alone time without fear. Somehow I had to value time that was not filled with a full calendar, socializing, and being around people—I had to stop connecting the idea of being alone with being rejected.

Honestly, the people I saw sitting at a restaurant eating alone or going to the movies solo always used to baffle me. My first instinct was to feel bad for them, because being alone must have meant they were a loner who didn't have friends, reliable family, or a significant other to spend time with.

But one day after discovering I had a chronic illness and autoimmune disease, my thought process started to shift. What if those people who sat alone weren't loners? What if it's a myth that spending time alone or doing things by ourselves makes us an outsider? What if I had the courage to do more things alone? What if I were comfortable enough with myself to spend quality time in the presence of my own company without judgment?

The first part of embracing my alone time made me face the reality that even if I was alone, it didn't have to mean I was *lonely*. Getting comfortable with just being with *me* meant I was brave, self-compassionate, and in touch with myself.

When I was living a fully packed social life, I craved attention and validation from everyone around me. In the process, I avoided contemplative time examining my own life and actions. In essence, I was looking to fill a void within by doing all the things and being all the things.

But what would it look like to truly live out this life of JOMO? How can we find a sense of connectedness from enjoying time in our own presence? And how can we do this without feeling overwhelming loneliness?

I'll never forget the first time I challenged myself to go to a movie alone. As a single woman, I knew a rom-com was out of the question and an action movie seemed too intense, so I settled for a warm-hearted family film with a beautiful message: *Wonder.* I knew it would be a tearjerker, so I took a pack of tissues, snuck in some comfort food (chocolate, of course), put on my most stretchy leggings, and walked into the AMC unsure of what to expect. As I approached the ticket counter, "All by Myself" by Celine Dion started blasting in my head, leading me to question why in my right mind I was publicly choosing to showcase my alone status.

Is this going to be awkward? Is everyone going to look at me and feel bad for me? Is it going to be terrible not to have someone else to experience the film with?

As I handed my ticket to an employee with these thoughts rushing through my mind, she looked at me and said, "Just you?" I paused and sheepishly said, "Yup, just me." I continued, "I'm taking myself on a date."

Yes, folks, I really said that. For a moment I was tempted to retract what may have come off as an incredibly dorky statement, but before I could, I took a breath, squashed the bubbling fear, smiled at her, and walked toward theater number 7. As corny as it sounded, I kind of liked the ring of taking myself on a date. I was going on a "Kait Date"—spending intentional quality time with myself. This wasn't an act of desperation; it was a powerful act of courage and bravery.

There is such profound power in reframing. Sometimes it requires only a second of mental clarity to take something your mind wants to see as a negative and turn it into something powerful, good, and glorious.

I walked into the theater and sat down in a middle seat, making note of the few people around me. As the movie progressed and the tears started streaming, I noticed something pretty amazing. Because I was all by myself, I felt like I could truly experience the movie. I felt like I could unashamedly feel *all* the feels. I could cry as much as I wanted, eat as much chocolate as my heart desired, and I could even put up the armrest to the seat next to me and sprawl out as comfortably as I wished (*#livingmybestlife*).

Going to the movie alone that day was a special experience. I walked out of the theater with an extra pep in my step, much like Elle Woods walking into Harvard Law.

Y'all, I did it!

I was freeing myself from the fears of loneliness and missing out and instead embracing the sweet, special moments of being alone. I had nothing to prove, whether I was at home by myself or with friends at a rooftop soiree.

Jesus Loved Alone Time

In late 2019, as I sat on top of the Mount of Beatitudes taking in the gorgeous pink flowers, the sparkling sunshine, and the peaceful view of the Sea of Galilee, I felt an overwhelming sense of fullness. I was alive, my soul was peaceful, my mind was rested. I thought, *Wow, this is why Jesus went away to pray so much. He was alone and yet fully connected to himself and to the Father.*

The New Testament is filled with accounts of Jesus going away to pray. Being alone wasn't scary to him; it was essential. He needed it for his mental, spiritual, emotional, and even physical well-being. It gave Jesus peace, it provided intentional time to pray and be with the Father, and it helped him process the things of the world with more space and clarity.

Sometimes we feel lonely because the relationships with ourselves and with God are the ones we crave most. We long to know ourselves and accept our unusual quirks and unique ways of seeing the world. We ache to see ourselves the way God sees us. We desperately want not to be afraid of the complexities of our own thoughts and reflections. We need space to truly and clearly process the weight of what is going on around us.

What was life like before we had smartphones to distract us while waiting in line for coffee? Do we even remotely remember what it was like to experience five minutes of boredom? How can we get back to true silence and solitude, which are both ultimately vital to our spiritual formation and human flourishing?

Too often we are looking to fill our core human needs through validation from others, keeping up with the culture, and even relentlessly defending our opinions. In doing this, we fail to realize we can also do all these things for ourselves. Spending intentional quality time with ourselves is an act of love that can heal us physically, emotionally, and even spiritually. But if we believe that space in our calendar or time by ourselves is a reflection of not being invited or wanted, we're missing out on something important, something that is, dare I say, magical.

> Spending intentional quality time with ourselves is an act of love that can heal us physically, emotionally, and even spiritually.

What I've found by consistently prioritizing and shifting my mindset about my alone time is that it actually makes me feel less alone in almost any situation. It now makes me feel powerful, it makes me feel loved, it makes me feel understood, and it makes me feel rested. In deeply embracing my me time and overcoming the myth of being alone, I no longer believe I am unworthy because I'm not around other people.

So, what if missing out isn't actually all that terrible?

Friend, many of us are getting it wrong by falling into the cultural norms and temptations of FOMO. Behind all the fear of missing out and the self-induced horror of facing alone time and the anxiety of loneliness is something special, sacred, and powerful. We are no less worthy without an invite or if we don't show up to something. In coming back to who we really are without all the noise of validation, all the doing, and all the busyness and constant yeses, a pure peace is waiting—a balanced, true connection to our gorgeous inner workings.

What if in fact all of this is actually necessary to truly live in the way of Jesus?

I don't know about you, but in the coming years, I plan to attend fewer events, simplify my schedule, say no more often, take intentional breaks from technology, and actively slim down my social calendar, all in exchange for prioritizing the simple space of settling into who I am and letting go of the need to prove my worth.

I'm giving up the fear of missing out and letting go of the angst I felt about alone time, and I'm trading it all in for a life that is more joyful, more simple, more resilient, more peaceful, and—I believe—more closely aligned with what Jesus intended.

That's the way I'm fighting for myself and what's important these days—settling into my true worth and refusing to buy the lie that who I am is wrapped up in some arbitrary number of calendar invites and a perfectly filled schedule. I've traded in my chock-full calendar for more noes and better boundaries as I daily see the fruit of alone time. Sure, some may say this new lifestyle seems a bit boring, but if living a life deeply interconnected with myself and with God is boring, then I'll take it.

Dear FOMO,

You once ruled my life and dictated how I showed up, what I did, and how many things I committed to. You caused me exhaustion, unnecessary anxiety, and a slew of health problems. But honestly, I'm proud to say you're old news now, my friend.

What I must thank you for, though, is that by trying to be at all the things and worrying about what I wasn't invited to, I realized that I was pushing away sacred time with myself and was as scared to say no as I was to be alone. Hitting a wall with you has forced me into a difficult but beautiful space of introspection. I've faced my fears of setting the boundaries I need, and I've started caring for myself and my own soul in deeply enriching ways.

I thank you for forcing me to discover the freeing gift of JOMO as I embrace my alone time in a beautiful, new, soul-filling way. Bring on the noes, the extra time to do fun things by myself and with God, and the sweet opportunities to find myself outside of external validation.

Some may say I'm a loner, while others may be disappointed by my new boundaries, but you know what? I know the truth, and I'm finally owning it proudly.

Yours Truly,
Kait

Remember These Things

- ➢ FOMO can slowly eat away at your health, your sense of your own worth and significance, and your ability to be present and satisfied in the moment.

- ➢ Going to fewer events means you can be present to more—more present with the current moment, more present with others, and even more present with yourself.

- ➢ If it's not a heck yes, it's a no.

- ➢ Being alone wasn't scary to Jesus; it was essential. He needed it for his mental, spiritual, emotional, and even physical well-being. It gave him peace, provided time to pray and be with the Father, and helped him process the things of the world with more space and clarity.

Ask These Things

- ➢ Honesty hour: Are you committing to things out of a fear of missing out? What are the lies you believe about missing out?

> How are you going to commit to saying no to more?

> Practically, how will you practice enjoying time in your own presence? Can you commit to rewriting the narrative of being alone?

Do These Things

> Write your own JOMO mission statement.

> Challenge yourself to do one thing this week fully and completely alone. Journal how you felt before and how you felt after. Get curious about your experience.

> Write a thank-you letter to FOMO.

CHAPTER 11

Is This Thing On?

Fighting the Silence of God

Miracles rarely happen on our time line. And you can't give God a deadline. But you can trust His timing. He's never early. He's never late. He's right on time, every time.

Mark Batterson

"Is there anyone out there? Can anybody hear me?"

Recognize where those lines are from? I'll give you a hint: giant ship, iceberg, love story.

If you immediately guessed *Titanic*, we are on the same wavelength, because that's my favorite movie of all time. You are clearly my people.

These lines are uttered in the movie after the ship sinks and one of the rescue boatmen is drifting through the icy waters filled with dead bodies, looking for any signs of life. It's a terribly bleak and depressing scene. It feels cold and void of hope.

I actually just googled how cold the water was in the Atlantic after the Titanic sank. Any guesses?

Guys. It was 28 degrees. For reference, the average pool is heated between 78 and 82 degrees Fahrenheit. Also, according to Google, at a temperature of 28 degrees, hypothermia starts in as quickly as fifteen minutes, and death happens in about thirty.

I cannot even begin to imagine what it would be like to try to stay afloat in water cold enough to kill me within minutes. I'm sorry to conjure up that kind of imagery in your mind, but there's a point here. If I'm being honest, sometimes I feel like this has been what my relationship with God looks like during my biggest moments of rejection.

When I'm in a season of feeling lost, confused, or pained, those moments of rejection often sting me the most. It's during those times that it seems everyone else all around me is receiving blessings, and I'm stuck trying to stay afloat on one half of a door in deathly ice-cold water. (Rose Dawson, I feel you, girl!)

I'll be praying for a breakthrough, only to hear silence.

I'll be asking God for help, only to feel nothing.

I'll be pressing into the thing I believe he's called me to, only to make virtually zero progress.

I'll experience something heart-shattering and feel angry at him for allowing it to happen. Or worse, right when I'm down and weak, something else hits my life, sending me into even further pain and grief. How could he allow any of it to happen?

It's discouraging, frustrating, and even flat-out angering at times.

In those moments, it can feel as though I'm crying out to God like that Titanic boatman cried out to the ship's survivors, saying, "God, are you out there? Can you hear me?"

Life is filled with all sorts of pain and rejection: people leaving us, people abusing us, people breaking our hearts, people betraying us, people not accepting us, people misunderstanding us. Then we also have to deal with our own personal rejections, like our deepest insecurities and inner self-hatred.

Through all this, God is *supposed* to be our constant. He is *supposed* to be our rock, our fortress. Our sense of safety and hiding place. Our ultimate shepherd and guide through times of trouble.

But what do we do when it seems God is totally silent? What do we do when our prayers are not being answered? What do we do when we're in the midst of life's biggest valleys and we feel like God's never going to provide a way out?

If I'm being honest, sometimes I've felt like God was rejecting me.

Did Someone Hit the Mute Button on God?

Maybe it's in the midst of a big decision I need to make.

Maybe it's within a long season of disappointments.

Maybe it's when I feel prompted to pray for something big, but then nothing happens.

Maybe it's when something unexplainable happens without any signs of it getting better.

In these moments, my prayers are unfiltered and raw. "God, for real? How long is this horribly painful and confusing season going to last? Why is it that I pray, pray, pray and keep feeling like nothing is happening? What are you doing up there? Why are you hiding from me?"

This shouldn't feel like a *Where's Waldo?* book! Yet there I am searching for answers, searching for guidance, searching to hear God's voice, but I can't seem to find him anywhere.

It's in these times that I often find myself filled with grief, lament, anger, and doubt. Usually nothing about the situation makes sense. After a time of tame frustration, if I feel like I'm not getting any answers, I'll often graduate to stage 2: screaming much like a fed-up toddler. I'll begin pleading with God.

"Listen, God, I need answers."

"Alright God, it's time you showed up right about now."

"Hey, God, I need to find a way out of this mess."

"Come on already, God. You need to make this right."

But the utter frustration doesn't seem to make God flinch. Despite all my concessions, on the other end of the line is the sound of . . . absolutely nothing at all. Just pure, uninterrupted silence.

"God, are you ghosting me? This is not the time for you to be like the 85 percent of guys I've met through online dating."

Sure, the distorted, broken world may reject me, but feeling like the God of the universe is ignoring me, misleading me, allowing pain to happen to me, or straight up rejecting me? That feels too hopeless and sickening to bear.

Keep Calling Out

I was in the sweet town of Arroyo Grande on California's Central Coast when I received a video message from my friend Kristie Christie (shout-out to Kristie! What a baller name, right?). Though I was trying to rid myself of distractions as I approached the deadline of the first draft of this manuscript, I felt prompted to open Kristie's video in our group text and listen to her message.

I was amazed at the words I heard next. Kristie (looking incredibly stunning in her Sunday best, I might add) said this to our group: "I think God wants to encourage you to see the trials that you are facing as an invitation to press in deeper into his spirit, to abide in him, and to trust in him. These testings and these difficult things are what he wants to use to strengthen you."

While this could've seemed like a pretty normal message we hear as Christians, I felt prompted to dig into how God might be using Kristie's words to speak to me as I was writing the pages of this chapter, facing the times I had felt abandoned by God.

Kristie's message immediately reminded me of James 1. I think we often have a love-hate relationship with James 1. We love it because it challenges us, but we hate it because, in essence, it says that hardship and pain can actually be good for us. Specifically, James 1:2–3 (ah, yes, I'm going there, folks) says, "Count it all joy, my brothers, when you meet trials of various kinds, for you know that the testing of your faith produces steadfastness" (ESV).

It goes on to say in verse 4, "And let steadfastness have its full effect, that you may be perfect and complete, lacking in nothing."

To me, the most jarring part about these verses is that the words *joy, trials,* and *steadfastness* appear to be connected in some way—which is not the easiest thing to think about when you are in the middle of a long-lasting, feel-like-my-life-is-over crisis.

But the word that's always stuck out the most from this verse is this: *steadfastness.*

I think it's mainly because this word seems a bit countercultural to how we do just about everything right now. I mean, we live in this modern era and have been conditioned for instant gratification.

Netflix to watch anything on demand at our fingertips (hello, *Grey's,* don't mind if I do).

DoorDash to deliver any food we are craving in minutes.

Uber to take us anywhere we want at the click of a button.

Amazon Prime to bring us almost anything at the lightning-fast speed of twenty-four to forty-eight hours (honestly, what did any of us do before Amazon Prime?).

Social media to post the extra trendy thing we are doing and get instant feedback via likes and comments.

Changing jobs when we've barely hit the one-year mark because we want to avoid even a tinge of boredom.

All these situations reinforce messaging that flashes end-lessly in our faces, saying, "Get whatever you want when you want it, and when you're not satisfied . . . peace out, onto the next!"

The problem is, we're receiving terrible training. We need to exert extreme effort to survive deep seasons of pain, confusion, and despair. We absolutely cannot just pray something once or twice, resolve to accept that God must not be listening to us, throw up our hands, and give up. Though it may not be the most popular opinion, we have to grip on to perseverance like it's our new BFF (Cher and Dionne style).

Maybe you are in the midst of a painful season where you feel as though God is totally ignoring you. You might be praying for clarity and direction, praying for a way through something challenging or painful, or praying for something big to happen. And you might be praying for days, weeks, months, maybe even years without actually seeing the fruit of your prayers. But here's where we need to shift our mentality. If whatever you're praying for doesn't happen right away, it doesn't mean God isn't listening. Maybe the answer isn't just for the situation to change. Maybe the answer isn't to know all the reasons why something is or is not happening. Maybe the answer is to truly trust that in the moments when we are faced with difficult trials and our faith is tested, clinging to prayer will yield something even greater: strength and steadfastness.

Everything tells us to get frustrated and discouraged when things aren't going our way or our prayers are not being answered or it seems so much easier for everyone else to find the clarity and direction they are looking for.

But what if instead of making it extra complicated for ourselves, we went on praying? What if we continued to place one foot in front of the other and kept returning to God in prayer? What if we allowed ourselves to lament? What if God wants us to take it back to one of the simplest acts of obedience?

One that shows, despite our difficult season, we are willing to continue to turn to God in our pain and doubt, trusting that he is truly with us.

We are called to persevere through prayer even when life gets not just hard but ridiculously hard. I'm talking climbing Mount Everest–type of excruciating here. We are called to keep praying even when it might seem impossible. Actually, *especially* when it seems impossible. We are called to trust, through faith, that even when we feel God is silent, he is still working behind the scenes.

In the Old Testament, specifically Numbers, we see how the Israelites continue to lack trust, faith, and obedience to God's plan and commands. Because the Israelites couldn't be patient, trust, and persevere in prayer, their temptation to take things into their own hands caused a forty-year delay.

> We are called to trust, through faith, that even when we feel God is silent, he is still working behind the scenes.

And we aren't talking forty minutes or forty days here. A journey that should have taken eleven days took forty years. We're talking forty years, people—*YEARS!*

Mark Batterson writes, "Miracles rarely happen on our time line. And you can't give God a deadline. But you can trust His timing. He's never early. He's never late. He's right on time, every time."[1]

I know long seasons of waiting, disappointment, grief, or confusion can be tiring, trying, and discouraging like no other . . . I hear you! But let's imagine what is truly more frustrating: (1) taking matters into our own hands and having it fail or even delay what God is trying to do; (2) trying to compartmentalize our pain now to bandage the issue, only to have it pop up later in a hurtful or destructive way; or (3) remaining patient and praying through the pains of waiting and healing (even if it means years) so that we grow in steadfastness and can truly appreciate the moment God reveals his great plans for the season we're in.

Here are some simple but powerful truths you can cling to in the moments you feel "rejected" by God (I recommend adding them to sticky notes and putting them everywhere you can see them):

- Even in the midst of your biggest valley, keep praying.
- Even when you don't think God is working at all, keep praying.
- Even when you don't think he can hear you, keep praying.
- Even when you are experiencing a boatload of adversity, keep praying.
- Even when you want to take matters into your own hands, resist. Keep praying.
- Even when it feels impossible, go right ahead and grab extra support but do *not* stop praying. Keep turning to God.

James goes on to say, "If any of you lacks wisdom, let him ask God, who gives generously to all without reproach, and it will be given him. But let him ask in faith, with no doubting, for the one who doubts is like a wave of the sea that is driven and tossed by the wind. For that person must not suppose that he will receive anything from the Lord; he is a double-minded man, unstable in all his ways" (James 1:5–8 ESV).

Though you might feel like the *Titanic* boatman drifting in that lifeboat, surrounded by cold, gloomy waters, *do not* stop calling out in steadfast prayer. Do not stop looking for even the slightest glimmer of life. Do not give up on building perseverance, but cling to the hope that God is *with* you through every moment of your greatest confusion and pain.

Hopeful Grieving

As we discuss the weight of feeling confused, frustrated, and even rejected by God, it's important that we also address how to healthily process these feelings. Now is the time where I have to address one of my biggest pet peeves. Sadly, I experience it most often in the church. And while I don't believe the intentions are necessarily bad, I do very much think it can do incredible damage if we don't start calling this thing out for what it is.

This *thing* I'm referring to is something I have found particularly damaging in navigating the unexpected and receiving silence from God. I like to refer to it as *toxic positivity*.

Toxic positivity is what we have been groomed to cling to in Western culture, as well as in many evangelical Christian communities. It's when we sometimes deny or gloss over our own pain or the pain of others with phrases like, "Don't worry, the best is yet to come" and "That's terrible! But don't forget, God is good." Though I believe God is good, and sure, the best may be yet to come, the issue with toxic positivity is that it does not leave space for our unkempt, raw emotions surrounding grief.

Life and its many situations are not all good or all bad. They are gray. But many of us don't like to live in the gray. The truth is, it's possible for us to grieve the moments we feel rejected in life while also simultaneously finding glimmers of hope to cling to. There is, by God's grace, a process to *grieve hopefully*.

In the process of grieving hopefully, I can believe that God is good and that he has good things in store for me, but I can simultaneously acknowledge the deep grief and pain that I'm feeling. I can choose to process these emotions rather than simply saying, "God is good" as a Band-Aid to suppress or deny them.

> There is, by God's grace, a process to *grieve hopefully.*

To learn how to do this, we must first talk about what it looks like to grieve. Grief itself is much more than *one* feeling. Elizabeth Kübler-Ross is widely known for her writings and thoughts on grief. In her book *On Death and Dying*, she discusses her theory of the five stages of grief called the Kübler-Ross Model. These are the five stages:

1. Denial
2. Anger
3. Bargaining
4. Depression
5. Acceptance[2]

But let's talk about the crux of the matter: Grief is anything but linear. One doesn't jump headfirst into denial and finish that stage forever, gracefully hop over to anger, and then after a little huffing and puffing, finish anger, slide their way into bargaining and so on until they reach the glorious stage of acceptance. Sadly, grief isn't the process of gracefully graduating from one stage to another like a student moving progressively through their schooling. That sure would be nice, but that's not how grief likes to function. If you've ever been aware of the process as you're grieving, you know as well as I do that it feels much more jarring and unpredictable.

Here's what grief often actually looks like: One day you feel incredibly sad and depressed, finding it hard to even get out of bed. The next day you feel a rush of anger toward a person, the situation, or God. Then a few days later you are hit by a wave of sadness again, tears streaming down your cheeks nonstop. But then, just maybe, one day you suddenly feel energized as though you're doing great, and you begin thinking, *Oh, I'm totally fine! I can do this whole grief thing. It's not that bad!* Until . . . guess what? Somethings triggers you, and desperation hits you like a ton of bricks, resulting in your bargaining and begging God to change your circumstances.

Grieving is messy and frustrating and never really resolves neatly and perfectly. But true beauty blooms when we surrender to the entire process—that's where the transformation is revealed.

I once heard Pastor John Mark Comer share in a sermon that "grieving isn't something that we do as much as it is something we let be done to us, let wash over us, that we surrender to."[3]

Some questions that now might be popping up for you are ones that my mind has gone to many times before: How do we grieve *hopefully*? How do we allow space for this ever-so-necessary process without suppressing our pain and cloaking ourselves with toxic positivity? How do we find something to hold on to that can help us to move forward?

Well, to make it through the journey, we need a sense of expectation. We need hope to cling to for the future. We need something that is constant . . .

> Grieving is messy and frustrating and never really resolves neatly and perfectly. But true beauty blooms when we surrender to the entire process—that's where the transformation is revealed.

something that is good and true . . . something that is exciting and beautiful. And I don't know about you, but the only thing I know of that embodies all those things combined is God himself.

Yes, the very thing we may be doubting or frustrated with is also the thing we can find our deepest hope within. You see, hope is not just wishful thinking. It's also not denying the bad and only speaking from a place of positivity. No, rather, hope is an expectation of goodness based on knowing the character of God and coming to terms with and surrendering to his promises.

Grieving means that as we lament and cry out to God with our steadfast prayers, we also set our hope in the confident expectation that God will work through it all because we understand his ultimate goodness and his beautiful promises throughout the Bible.

Don't believe me? I have a better source for you. The New Testament is filled with all kinds of hope:

We boast in the hope of the glory of God. (Rom. 5:2)

Not only so, but we also glory in our sufferings, because we know that suffering produces perseverance; perseverance, character; and character, hope. (Rom. 5:3–4)

But if we hope for what we do not see, we wait for it with patience. (Rom. 8:25 ESV)

Praise be to the God and Father of our Lord Jesus Christ! In his great mercy he has given us new birth into a living hope through the resurrection of Jesus Christ from the dead. (1 Pet. 1:3)

The hope here is not that nothing bad will ever happen to us again—Jesus never promised that. In fact, he promised the opposite when he said, "In this world you will have trouble" (John 16:33). Our hope can't be self-righteous. Just because we endured our worst rejection doesn't mean we are immune to pain and God will never allow another bad thing to happen to us ever again. No, we are literally supposed to expect suffering. It's part of being human.

Now, don't get me wrong. It's not as though God is sitting on his throne somewhere high up in the clouds, excited about the pain we are going through. In fact, knowing the sweet, loving, tender, gracious character of his Son, Jesus, proves to me that God doesn't want us to be this grieved. In fact, he hurts when we hurt.

The hope that remains in our time of grief is this: God is at work in our hearts and souls, and he will use our pain to help transform us beautifully for the good of this world.

> God is at work in our hearts and souls, and he will use our pain to help transform us beautifully for the good of this world.

Now, that's a hopeful promise we can sink into. That's how we can move toward the path of hopeful grieving.

But How?

Through all the rejections I've experienced, I was finally able to put this concept to the test after my heartbreak with Chris. I truly could not make sense of that breakup and had no idea on God's green earth why he would let something so devastating happen to me.

But instead of turning from God or blaming him or insisting on knowing the why, I turned instead to prayer and hopeful grieving.

This meant giving myself permission to cry and be as frustrated as ever, while also still having a clear grasp of hope. I lamented like crazy that season with God. I let the grief happen to me. And I let it happen to me, believing that God was with me in my fear, anger, tears, and bargaining. I clung to a trust that God was transforming the pain into something beautiful.

In his sermon "Praying Our Tears," Tim Keller talks about bringing all our tears to God.[4] Psalm 39:12 says,

> Hear my prayer, O LORD,
>   and give ear to my cry;
> hold not your peace at my tears! (ESV)

I love this because it gives us permission to let it rip—cry, scream, yell, beg, question. We have permission to bring all of our messy, unkempt selves to God whenever we want and as often as we want. We can pray our tears and our pains and our frustrations in all of our grief. He is listening. Don't stop—keep going. Put more energy into your tank and keep pushing against the wall that's trying to keep you stuck and block you from processing this grief. Keep pushing past the confusion that's flooded with fears. Don't let any of it stop you from crying out to him in your darkest hour. Bring the frustrations you have to God in prayer. Tell him you are struggling to feel any hope. Ask him for his loving hope to be sealed in your heart.

And if you don't feel relieved or experience a glimmer of hope at first, try again. And again. And again. And again. Experiencing all the stages of grief with God is vital for deep healing and true revelation.[5]

During my grieving season, I also went on daily worship walks where the Hillsong tune "Hosanna" became my anthem. I would allow myself time to pray, "Lord, heal my heart and make it clean. Open my eyes to the things unseen."

I also journaled. A lot. I have found journaling to be a beautiful tool for releasing my emotions. There's something about opening a fresh journal, taking good old-fashioned pen to paper, and scribbling my way through the processing of my innermost head and heart.

I guess science agrees with me, because writing to process pain has been proven to help the healing process. In fact, it is more beneficial to write with a pen and paper than to type on a phone or computer. Journaling helps us get the emotions out of our bodies. Needless to say, in my hopeful grieving, I journaled like a wild woman.

I also wrote phrases of hope on sticky notes and placed them in spots I'd see every day. I stuck them in my bathroom, on my computer, on my desk, on my bedroom mirror, even in my car. These hopeful slips of paper created small moments to redirect my focus away from the downward spiral I was tempted to slide down and instead redirect toward the hopeful promise that God was with me and would make something beautiful out of my pain.

Another essential practice I implemented was doing one fun thing for myself every week. Throughout our moments of grief, it's especially important to be kind and loving to ourselves. The season of heartache after Chris and I broke up is when I decided to get a season pass to Disneyland. It ended up being one of the only places I could truly experience authentic, soul-filling joy. Maybe for you it's a weekly adventure or a night of pampering or spending quality time with a few of your most cherished sisters. It's special and vital during our pain processing to give ourselves little hugs of comfort, joy, and love.

Hard days of grief progressively began to give way to days and then weeks of strength and only small moments of grief. Months went by as I grew stronger and found solace in God's loving presence and a deep hope that he both was with me and would make beauty from ashes. By shifting my focus from the *why* to the hopeful promises of *what* God was doing in my life in the moment and what he would do in the future,

By shifting my focus from the *why* to the hopeful promises of *what* God was doing in my life in the moment and what he would do in the future, I regained strength.

I regained strength. Piece by piece, I saw the tattered parts of my broken heart being glued back together.

I wonder, what can you do to press into hopeful grieving? What things can you add to your season of pain to provide space to process your feelings and go through the stages of grief? How can you bring God into the process like your intimate bestie? And what can you do for yourself that's extra loving and kind to your heart?

Hopeful grieving is possible for us all.

In *Titanic*, when Rose is on the brink of freezing to death, she has a choice to make. She can sit on that door and await the inevitability of impending death. After all, she's just lost the love of her life and is cold and nearly lifeless. That would be the easy way in the midst of pain and unthinkable grief.

But then she remembers the promise she made to her dying love just moments before. Jack said, "You must do me this honor. You must promise me that you'll survive. That you won't give up, no matter what happens, no matter how hopeless. Promise me now, Rose, and never let go of that promise. Never let go." And Rose promised him, "I'll never let go, Jack."[6]

Instead of giving up, Rose gets off that door, begins swimming in the chilling water, and valiantly blows a whistle to get the attention of the boatman.

She has just lost the man she loves, but she chooses to cling to the promise she made. She grasps on to hope. As she hears Jack's voice in her ear, she feels the confidence that she can be okay if she just pushes through. Her steadfastness shines.

She persists by facing the horror of the moment and clinging to the hope of new life. She blows that whistle as though it is a desperate prayer. She grasps on to perseverance and clings to hope. And because of that, she goes on to live a full and beautiful life.

And, friend, you can too.

Dear God,

Honestly, writing a letter to you is hard because there are so many things I want to say. So, I'll just start with the most obvious: I love you. Maybe I should have eased my way into that, but it's truer than anything I know.

I love you despite all my doubt. Even through all the trials. Even when I've felt you haven't been listening. Even when I thought I was all alone. Even in my hardest moments of grief.

I realize now that I've never really been all alone. You've always been listening to me and loving me. I can see now that you've always been at work in my heart and soul. You've been intricately and uniquely molding me for the good of this world.

Thank you for your mercy when I felt I didn't deserve it. Thank you for hearing my prayers, even if the answer wasn't immediate. Thank you for being patient with me, even when I wasn't being patient with you. Thank you for always providing a hopeful way forward in the moments I felt lost about where I was headed. Thank you for your love when I needed it most.

You are good, you are love, you are my God.

Yours Truly,
Kait

Remember These Things

> You can't just pray something once or twice, resolve to accept that God must not be listening to you, and then give up. You need strength and steadfastness in times of waiting.

> You can believe God is good and has good things planned for you while simultaneously acknowledging the depths of the grief and pain that you're feeling. You can choose to process grief and pain rather than just saying "God is good" as a Band-Aid to suppress or deny the emotions you're facing.

> The hope that remains in your time of grief is this: God is at work in your heart and soul, and he will use your pain to help transform you beautifully for the good of this world.

Ask These Things

> What can you do to be consistent and steadfast in your prayer life?

> In what ways have you grown weary or tried to take matters into your own hands?

> Have you ever dabbled in the waters of toxic positivity? How can you break this cycle in your life or put boundaries up when it's happening to you?

> What can you do to practically press into hopeful grieving?

Do These Things

> Identify the top three prayers you want to bring to God about past or present confusion, pain, or disappointment.

> Write a hopeful grieving plan filled with things that are extra loving and kind to your heart.

> Write a thank-you letter to God.

Conclusion

This Is Me

I can be changed by what happens to me. But I refuse
to be reduced by it.

Maya Angelou

Rejection.

How does it feel reading that word now? Is it maybe a little
less scary?

We all have notes of it strung along in our story—whether
abuse, betrayal, sexual shame, not fitting in, being uninvited,
being told no, or even the brutal stings of our own self-rejections
that come in the dangerous forms of self-hate and stifling insecurity. These rejections can keep us small and scared. They
can destroy every ounce of goodness within us, even paralyze
us from moving forward. *Or* they can become things we grow
through, learn from, and one day claim as victory.

Which story do you want to live?

Don't get me wrong. Sometimes I still break down crying. Sometimes I feel overwhelmed, with triggers causing a tailspin of anxious thoughts. Sometimes the rebellious parts of my inner child decide she wants to rule my emotions and actions for the day. Sometimes I let her. Sometimes I'm tempted to stay in bed rather than face another day where the risk of rejection feels too great.

These rejections can keep us small and scared.

But more and more, I'm learning balance. I'm learning that life is filled with tons of dualities—pain and happiness, destruction and healing, chaos and peace—but for the first time, I'm not as afraid. I'm allowing myself to feel the pain of past rejections when they surface. I'm facing present-day troubles with more courage and calming my fears of the unknown in the future. I'm asking God for the grace to handle each day as it comes, day by day.

I picture all these emotions packed together, like little kids riding their very own pink school bus (I'm just not much of a yellow girl, what can I say?). In the back of the bus is surprise (she likes to feel a surge of excitement as the bus hops over bumps), in the middle you'll find disgust and anger, and closer to the front, just close enough to constantly whisper in my ear, are fear and sadness. There they are, the emotional gang, all making their home in the brown faux-leather seats of my moving pink box, shouting their opinions and competing for my attention. It's also important to note who's at the front of the bus. In the passenger seat, there's my inner child—the precious parts of my soul. It's good to have her close by; I'm done hiding her and shaming her, after all. But even still, it's important that she stays in the passenger seat. There I can make sure she feels heard, knowing she doesn't have the power to drive the bus forward. I mean, can you imagine a child driving a big bus?

And up in the driver's seat, there I am. I've got both hands on the wheel, and I'm pushing my foot against the gas pedal, motivated by the beautiful force that allows us all to truly live: God's inherent love. What I've learned in processing the hardships of life is that my emotions and my inner child are all welcome on the bus. I'm done trying to keep them small, and what they have to say is important. But I'm also not about to let them consume me entirely. I've learned that all are welcome to ride, but the only one who's allowed to drive is me, motivated by love.

That's my hope and my prayer for you too, friend.

You're going to experience the fear of rejection. When you hear the emotion of fear blazing in your ear, telling you to never engage in another relationship again because it's too risky, listen to her and hear her concern. And when she's done blaring, thank her for trying to protect you but turn your ear away and keep pressing forward in love.

This is how you live a life with the unknown of future rejection. Know that rejection is inevitable; it will come, as well as all the emotions along with it, but you can choose to let only love be the driving force in your life.

When you're driving with love and wise trust, you can find compassion for yourself and others. You can find joy even amid the sadness. You can find courage to fight for yourself. And you can turn your pain into purpose.

Have you ever truly shared your story from the pain of your past rejections?

Maybe your pastor asked you to share your testimony.

Or you were asked to talk in front of a group of people.

Or a friend put you on the spot at a dinner in front of others.

Or maybe you just shared it with your dog.

No matter what the scenario, I think we can all admit it takes some major courage, doesn't it?

I remember the last time I felt insanely afraid of putting my story out there for the world to hear. It was the evening before I recorded a conversation with my friend Mike Foster on his well-known podcast, *Fun Therapy*. If you're thinking, *FUN Therapy?* . . . Yes, I said *fun.* I know it seems counterintuitive, but when you have someone so gentle and kind that he embodies the essence of Mr. Rogers himself, it surprisingly is a bit fun. Not to mention, under all the layers of grime and shame and pain is truly so much beauty. On the opposite end of shame, love is waiting for us.

Over dinner the night before the *Fun Therapy* interview, I asked Mike if he had any tips for me. I kept focusing on what I could do to be different from other guests to make sure I sounded just the right amount of hurt yet hopeful. I was dialed in on what to say to be accepted, to be remembered, to be admired until he said this: "Kait, don't sugarcoat your pain. Just show up exactly as you are with whatever you have felt and share whatever you have learned. Your realness will be the gift that helps others do the same."

I looked at him, half smiled, and sheepishly replied, "Sounds good, Mike." I knew exactly what he was talking about, yet I was terrified. He meant I needed to reveal the brutal truth about my pain and my past while also being honest about the fact that I'm still working through some things. I had to fight my urge to tie every sentence with a silver bow. I had to be painstakingly honest with myself in front of God knows how many listeners, surrendering my temptation to "manage my image."

It takes insane bravery to share the rejections that have marred us with intense pain. It also takes equal amounts of courage to reveal our arduous journey of healing. But you know what takes double the courage? Being able to admit we are still working through some lingering thoughts and facing present-day battles. Fighting for balance amid all the feelings on the bus vying for our attention is a noble journey.

I left the dinner, went to my little Airbnb in Oceanside, sat on the bed, and hit play on a Sleeping at Last song about Enneagram type 3s, and reflected on Mike's words. I let every word sink in as it looped over and over again, letting the phrases become my anthem. I wanted to see an image of my brokenness utterly worthy of love. But how? I wanted to embrace what is real, letting my heart feel what it feels. But was that possible? I wanted to stand brave as I put my greatest failures on display, worthy of love anyway. But could I?

The next morning, I put on a cream-and-black bohemian chic dress, red lipstick, and a cute, flat-brimmed straw hat with a black ribbon I bought in Tuscany. I joined Mike in a room filled with windows that smelled like fresh paper. He handed me a small mic to attach to my dress, placed tissues at our side, looked at me with a calming smile, and said, "You can do this Kait. I'm so proud of you."

I breathed a deep this-is-it sigh, and he hit record.

Months later when the podcast went live, I felt a surge of fear. Every time I heard the clamoring noises of my emotions saying, *They're going to hate your story, You could have done better, You're a hot mess and now everyone knows it,* I made a choice. Instead of letting the emotions drive my pink bus and crash me into a terrible pit or lead me down a dangerous path, I thanked them for their concern and instead kept my hands on the wheel, choosing love.

I went outside, opened my phone to the podcast, and hit play as I walked around my neighborhood on that brisk January day. I listened as I talked about my biggest heartbreak and my biggest lies of heartbreak and thought, *Whew, that was courageous.* I continued to listen as I exposed some of my still-lingering shame from my past abuse. *Man, I can't believe I just admitted to that—I was really brave.* I listened for longer as I heard myself choking back tears and admitting to Mike that I still struggle with being a single woman so wounded by the rejection of numerous men.

When the interview ended, I stopped, smiled, looked up, and let the radiance of the sun dry the wet tears off my face, and then I thought, *I did it.*

What came next shocked my soul and burst my heart into a billion pieces.

Thousands of people listened. I was stunned. Then something even more marvelous happened: I started getting messages directly from people. One message turned into two, turned into ten, turned into one hundred, turned into hundreds. I received hundreds upon hundreds of messages from strangers sharing how they saw themselves in my pain, how they had been through similar rejections, and how they were also still working to pick back up some of their own pieces.

My soul felt entirely exposed while simultaneously loved and accepted. What a healing gift. I don't even think I realized how much my soul needed this. All the deep reflection, the processing, the pain, the healing, the bravery to get back up after being knocked down on my face. I realized after the launch of that interview that in certain ways, I needed some of these rejections to happen. Maybe not all of them, especially the horrifically abusive ones. But now I see them all, and without judgment or hatred, I look at them. I see the brutality, the betrayal, the frustration, the sadness, the shame, and the pain, and all I want to do is wrap them up in my arms and squeeze them tight. They don't seem as big or as daunting anymore. They're smaller, more healed, more manageable.

And now, tapping into my courage to write this book has exposed me to deeper depths of healing I didn't even know I could venture to. As strange as it might seem to be thankful for seasons of suffering, layers of shame, and all the lies and fears brought on by rejection, I've come to realize that I truly am. Because finally, I've been able to find what's underneath—the true *me*.

Friend, maybe you aren't going to write a book or do a public interview. Maybe you'll do something simple yet beautifully profound. Maybe pressing into the unknown and facing your biggest life rejections has allowed you to now have empathy for the woman who has been through a rejection similar to yours. Maybe you'll be the perfect shoulder and listening ear she needs in her darkest hour, and that will be the exact gift that she needed to not feel alone.

Or maybe processing your deepest rejection has given you the courage to start owning your body in a bikini without makeup and help others do the same.

Or maybe it's allowed you to finally connect to your inner child and give others permission to experience similar child-like wonder.

Or maybe it's made you have a keen eye to spot when someone may be in a potentially harmful relationship and to be the help she needs.

But if you get stuck thinking that your rejections have tainted you, or if you get lost in a downward tailspin trying to understand why the terrible pains of your past happened, you'll miss out.

Don't miss out on the divine beauty that awaits because all you can see is your disappointments.

I went from being on that podcast to publishing this book, which is easily now the most exposing thing I've ever done in my life. Filling pages with my most vulnerable, traumatic, heartbreaking stories for people to read? Years ago, that would have sounded like my worst nightmare.

> Don't miss out on the divine beauty that awaits because all you can see is your disappointments.

And at this point, you may love it, you may hate it, but neither of those things really matter. Actually, for those who don't like it, I'll just go ahead and say this: *thank you for rejecting me* (the irony, right?). Because the victory alone is in having the courage to heal from our past and to speak about it.

Sharing about how I processed and found purpose in my biggest rejections isn't about my throwing it in your face saying, "I can do this, and you can't." The point is the opposite. My broken, lost, tattered self was able to muster up even an ounce of courage and strength to commit to doing it. I *know* that you can too.

I hope today is the day you finally see yourself in all the brokenness, knowing you are (and have always been) so worthy of love.

I pray this is the day you take a stand against your past rejections to say, "Painful rejections have happened to me, and while they've hurt like crazy, they won't stop me from getting back on my feet, fighting for myself, and finding purpose in the pain."

Here's what I have to say to all my past rejections:

Dear Rejection,

Thank you for rejecting me. Because of you, I am moving into something more beautiful. Because of you, I've been able to experience the depths of deep emotion and the peaks of true joy. Because of you, I've discovered how to embrace my emotions, my inner child and deepest part of my soul, all of me. Because of you, I've been able to more deeply and truly connect to others with a compassion and empathy I never knew before. Because of you, I now know you, and I anticipate you, and I have more grit and tenacity and endurance to face you. Because of you, I've healed, I've been set free, I've become more whole. Because of you, I have something to courageously share to make others feel more seen, more known, and more loved.

Even though I won't voluntarily sign up to face you again, I know it might happen, but this time I'm ready. This time I'm stronger. This time I'm showing up loved.

Thank you for rejecting me. It's made me exactly who I am today.

Yours Truly,
Kait

I hope today is the day you claim this for yourself too.

Acknowledgments

The mere fact that these words have been written feels like an impossibility, but I know without a shadow of a doubt that it never would have been possible without my friends, my family, my HOD Community, and, of course, my Jesus empowering me on this journey.

For my amazing brother, Brandon Warman. You were the first person to believe in *Heart of Dating*. When I was terrified to step out into this vulnerable mission, you reinforced that what I had to say mattered. Your faith in me gave me the push I needed to enter into teaching in this ever-so-ambiguous world of Christian dating. Without your encouragement years ago, I wouldn't be where I am now. Your advocacy, love, and friendship have been so healing to my heart.

For my beautiful mother, Janice Warman. You always tell me I am beautiful, smart, and loved and can do anything I want to. Well, Mom, your daughter wrote a book! You've always been my number one fan, willing to shout how proud you are of me from any rooftop. You've been through the worst and back, and you've sacrificed so much to raise me and Brandon.

You've taught me so much, and I don't know how to truly thank you for your continual support. Through many of the seasons shared in this book, you have been my very best friend.

For my father, David Warman. Dad, I love you so much. You are extremely kind and have such a tender, loving heart. You are one of the most intelligent men I've ever met. I owe so much of the smarts I have to your stellar brainy genes. You are incredibly important to me.

For my stepmom, Karin. You are very thoughtful and kind, and you always make me feel special. Love you big.

To Grandma and Grandpa Powers, your example and legacy live in my memories. You both taught me about relationships through the way you love.

A special thank you to my best friend and fellow author, Kristen Perino (Merjanian), for believing in me, encouraging me on every step of the journey, and sacrificially reading every single page of this book before I sent it to my editor. Sister, you truly lived this entire journey, step-by-step, with me. I couldn't be more grateful for you.

For all my other amazing sister girlfriends, Nika Diwa, Sarah Kurtenbach, Meki Blackwell, Kathleen Rodgers, Kat Hennessey, Jessica Chow, Jessica Shakir, and Ali Motroni. You girls are truly like my very own living and breathing real-life sisters. Thank you for the continuous texts of encouragement. For the affirmations that make me come alive and feel understood. Thank you for always coming into the trenches with me, praying alongside me, and helping me stand on my own two feet after every knockdown. Lord knows a girl needs an army of sisters around her when she goes through life's worst rejections. You girls have been a huge comfort and source of judgment-free love in my life. Each of you inspires me. I love you so much.

Thank you to Lizzie Jones, my amazing mentor and good friend, for guiding me, grooming me, and growing me in wisdom.

Thank you to my incredible agent, Alex Fields. This wouldn't have happened without you first finding me, believing in my story, and fighting for me.

Thank you to Rachel Jacobson, my wonderfully patient and gracious editor, who made me feel like a million bucks this entire journey. Rachel, you deserve an award for being extremely patient every single time I threw a tantrum and wanted to give up (which was often). Not only that, but thank you to the entire Baker Books family for investing in this whirlwind of a book. We did it!

Thank you to my amazing, one-of-a-kind assistant, Gabriella Aspuru. You picked up so much of the slack throughout this entire journey. You worked late nights, dealt with my discombobulated thoughts and ideas, and helped keep *Heart of Dating* afloat as I fiercely ran full speed ahead after my dreams. Above that, you care deeply about relationships and believe in me. I'm so grateful for you.

Thank you to all the amazing pastors, friends, and just simply wonderful people who have poured into me on this journey: Casey Helmick, Whitney Gossett, Kat Harris, Stephanie May Wilson, Mike Foster, Debra Fileta, Bianca Olthoff, Hannah Brencher, Lauren Scruggs, Jonathan Pokluda, Allie Trowbridge, Cheryl Scruggs, Rashawn Copeland, Eryn Eddy, Ashley Abercrombie, Dr. Margaret Nagib, Scott Karrow, Dr. Celeste Holbrooke, Kristie Christie, Nathan Clarkson, Jamal and Natasha Miller, Brittney Moses, Addison Bevere, Juli Bevere, Alec Bevere, Carrie-Rose Menocal, Jessica Kelly, Allee Williams, Monica Zuniga, Jayme Thompson, Kelsey Chapman, Asis Almonte, Hannah Gronowski, Gabrielle Odom, Jeanette Tapley, Adam Weber, Meshali Mitchell, Dr. Therese Mascardo, Toni Collier, Carrie Lloyd, Jamie Grace, Chad Gamble, Brian and Lexi Cole, Scott Kedersha, Ger Jones, Katie Bulmer, and so many others! This book was a labor of love, conquering some of the biggest peaks and valleys I've ever experienced all in the span of a year and a half. You guys helped me finish it. I love you all.

And finally, to my Jesus. You are the miracle worker of them all. Because of you, I have healed and broken free of so much pain. Because of you, I am seen, heard, known, and loved. You have stirred up a courage I never knew I had inside of me. May everything I do be done out of my love for you. Here's to you, best friend.

Introduction

1. Inspired by Ariana Grande, "Thank U, Next," 2019, track 11 on *Thank U, Next* (Republic Records, 2019), CD.

Chapter 1 Neon Bikinis and Cellulite

1. Hillary McBride, *Mothers, Daughters, and Body Image* (Brentwood, TN: Post Hill Press, 2017), ix.

Chapter 2 Here I Am

1. Brené Brown, *The Gifts of Imperfection: Let Go of Who You Think You're Supposed to Be and Embrace Who You Are* (Center City, MN: Hazelden, 2010), 49.
2. Christopher K. Germer, *The Mindful Path to Self-Compassion: Freeing Yourself from Destructive Thoughts and Emotions* (New York: Guilford Press, 2009), 35.

Chapter 3 Never Have I Ever

1. Josh Harris, *I Kissed Dating Goodbye* (Colorado Springs: Multnomah Books, 2003).
2. Jonathan Grant, *Divine Sex: A Compelling Vision for Christian Relationships in a Hypersexualized Age* (Grand Rapids: Brazos Press, 2015), 10.
3. Linda Kay Klein, *Pure: Inside the Evangelical Movement That Shamed a Generation of Young Women and How I Broke Free* (New York: Atria Books, 2018).
4. Klein, *Pure*, 14.
5. Brené Brown, *Daring Greatly: How the Courage to Be Vulnerable Transforms the Way We Live, Love, Parent, and Lead* (New York: Avery, 2012), 75.
6. Klein, *Pure*, 27–28.

Chapter 4 Sorry, Not Sorry

1. Lauren Weisberger, *The Devil Wears Prada* (New York: Broadway Books, 2003), 91.

2. Brené Brown, *Braving the Wilderness: The Quest for True Belonging and the Courage to Stand Alone* (New York: Random House, 2019), 157.

3. Christina Grimmie, "Confidence is not 'they will like me.' Confidence instead is 'I'll be fine if they don't,'" Twitter, January 14, 2015, 4:05 p.m., https://twitter.com/therealgrimmie/status/555470759200432128?lang=en.

4. Jessica Cumberbatch Anderson, "Maya Angelou Opens Women's Health and Wellness Center, Calls Disparities 'Embarrassing,'" HuffPost, May 16, 2012, https://www.huffpost.com/entry/maya-angelou-opens-womens-health-center-calls-disparities-embarrassing_n_1517418?ref=black-voices.

Chapter 5 The Ugly Cry

1. Megan Laslocky, "This Is Your Brain on Heartbreak," *Greater Good Magazine*, February 15, 2013, https://greatergood.berkeley.edu/article/item/this_is_your_brain_on_heartbreak.

2. Dr. Caroline Leaf, "You Are Not a Victim of Your Biology!" Dr. Leaf, October 3, 2018, https://drleaf.com/blogs/news/you-are-not-a-victim-of-your-biology.

3. Leaf, "You Are Not a Victim."

4. Krista Tippett, "Brené Brown: Strong Back, Soft Front, Wild Heart," *On Being*, February 8, 2018, https://onbeing.org/programs/brene-brown-strong-back-soft-front-wild-heart/.

Chapter 6 Now You See Me, Now You Don't

1. Darlene Lancer, JD, LMFT, "Are You Stuck in a Cycle of Abandonment?" *Psychology Today*, August 13, 2019, https://www.psychologytoday.com/us/blog/toxic-relationships/201908/are-you-stuck-in-cycle-abandonment.

2. Susan Anderson, *Black Swan: The Twelve Lessons of Abandonment Recovery* (New York: Rock Foundations Press, 1999), 25–29.

3. Bessel A. van der Kolk, *The Body Keeps the Score: Brain, Mind, and Body in the Healing of Trauma* (New York: Penguin, 2014), 102–3.

4. Van der Kolk, *The Body*, 103.

5. Jennie Allen, *Get Out of Your Head: Stopping the Spiral of Toxic Thoughts* (Colorado Springs: Waterbrook, 2020), 63.

Chapter 7 The Dreaded F-Word

1. Mark Emmons, "Key Statistics About Millennials in the Workplace," Dynamic Signal, accessed July 16, 2020, https://dynamicsignal.com/2018/10/09/key-statistics-millennials-in-the-workplace/.

2. Thomas Merton, *New Seeds of Contemplation* (New York: New Directions, 2007), 34.

3. Jon Tyson, *The Burden Is Light: Liberating Your Life from the Tyranny of Performance and Success* (Colorado Springs: Multnomah, 2018), 5.

4. As quoted in Tim Keller, *Every Good Endeavor: Connecting Your Work to God's Work* (New York: Penguin, 2012), xix.

Chapter 8 I'm Not Crazy

1. National Domestic Violence Hotline, "Get the Facts & Figures," accessed August 27, 2020, https://www.thehotline.org/resources/statistics/.

2. Sydney Martin, "Eliminate That Seven Times Statistic: How to Stay Away for Good," Break the Silence Against Domestic Violence, January 15, 2017, https://breakthesilencedv.org/beat-that-seven-times-statistic/.

3. Pamela Dussault Runtagh, "How to Avoid Emotionally Abusive Relationships," HuffPost, September 21, 2013, https://www.huffpost.com/entry/how-to-avoid-emotionally-_b_3631367.

4. "Celine Dion Is Amazing," posted March 23, 2008, YouTube video, 3:50, https://www.youtube.com/watch?v=CEggoXwoXEY.

5. Runtagh, "How to Avoid Emotionally Abusive Relationships."

6. National Domestic Violence Hotline, "Get the Facts & Figures."

7. Runtagh, "How to Avoid Emotionally Abusive Relationships."

Chapter 10 All by Myself

1. John Mark Comer, *The Ruthless Elimination of Hurry: How to Stay Emotionally Healthy and Spiritually Alive in the Chaos of the Modern World* (Colorado Springs: WaterBrook, 2019), 39.

2. Tonya Dalton, *The Joy of Missing Out: Live More by Doing Less* (Nashville: Thomas Nelson, 2019).

Chapter 11 Is This Thing On?

1. Mark Batterson, *The Grave Robber: How Jesus Can Make Your Impossible Possible* (Grand Rapids: Baker Books, 2015), 89.

2. Elizabeth Kübler-Ross, *What the Dying Have to Teach Doctors, Nurses, Clergy, and Their Own Families* (New York: Scribner, 1997), 274.

3. John Mark Comer, "Hope in a Time of Disappointment" (sermon, Bridgetown Church, Portland, OR, delivered on April 19, 2020), https://bridgetown.church/teaching/house-to-house/hope-in-a-time-of-disappointment/.

4. Tim Keller, "Praying Our Tears," February 27, 2000, YouTube video, posted August 10, 2015, https://www.youtube.com/watch?v=DxOWWWVDGD0.

5. Wayne Jonas, MD, "15 Journaling Exercises to Help You Heal, Grow, and Thrive," *Psychology Today*, November 15, 2018, https://www.psychologytoday.com/us/blog/how-healing-works/201811/15-journaling-exercises-help-you-heal-grow-and-thrive.

6. *Titanic*, directed by James Cameron (1997, Los Angeles: Paramount, 1999), DVD.

About the Author

Kait Warman is a Los Angeles–based relationship coach, online educator, speaker, and host of the *Heart of Dating* podcast. Her mission is to empower men and women to have the courage to own their story, walk in victory, thrive with purpose, and discover clarity and vision in their lives and relationships.

She loves Jesus, going to Disneyland as much as possible, and all things French, and she is wildly obsessed with Celine Dion. Kait believes each person is perfectly unique, loved, and worthy of God's best, but we all need to remember to dance it out just a bit more. This is her first book.

Connect with Kait

 @kaitness

Unmask the ever-so-ambiguous world of dating

Join host Kait Warman as she seeks to start a healthy conversation with men and women and provide wise input by answering tough questions and uncovering transformative ways to develop a healthy attitude and approach to dating as a Christian.

 @Heartofdating

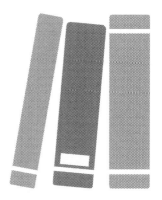

LIKE THIS
BOOK?
Consider sharing
it with others!

- Share or mention the book on your social media platforms. Use the hashtag **#TYFRM**.

- Write a book review on your blog or on a retailer site.

- Pick up a copy for friends, family, or anyone who you think would enjoy and be challenged by its message!

- Share this message on Twitter, Facebook, or Instagram: **I loved #TYFRM by @kaitness // @ReadBakerBooks**

- Recommend this book for your church, workplace, book club, or class.

- Follow Baker Books on social media and tell us what you like.

    ReadBakerBooks

    ReadBakerBooks

    ReadBakerBooks

Printed in the United States
By Bookmasters